THE INCA TRAIL TO MACHU PICCHU
The sacred route

All rights reserved
Hilbert Sumire
First edition May 2021

Urbanization Cristo Pobre Lot D - 2, Cusco Cell. 948001871
E-mail: hilbertsumire@gmail.com

© Photo credits: Thierry Jamin, Cody Sherrill, Ismael Uscachi, Kellyn Rojas, Francisco Huarcaya, Wilfredo Farfan
© Sketch: Charly Cárdenas © Maps: Michel Sumire

Layout and design: Alain Bonnet

N° ISBN: 9798541379631

Reproduction of all or part of the graphic features of this book by any means without
the permission of the author is prohibited

Cusco - Peru
2021

THE INCA TRAIL TO MACHU PICCHU
The sacred route

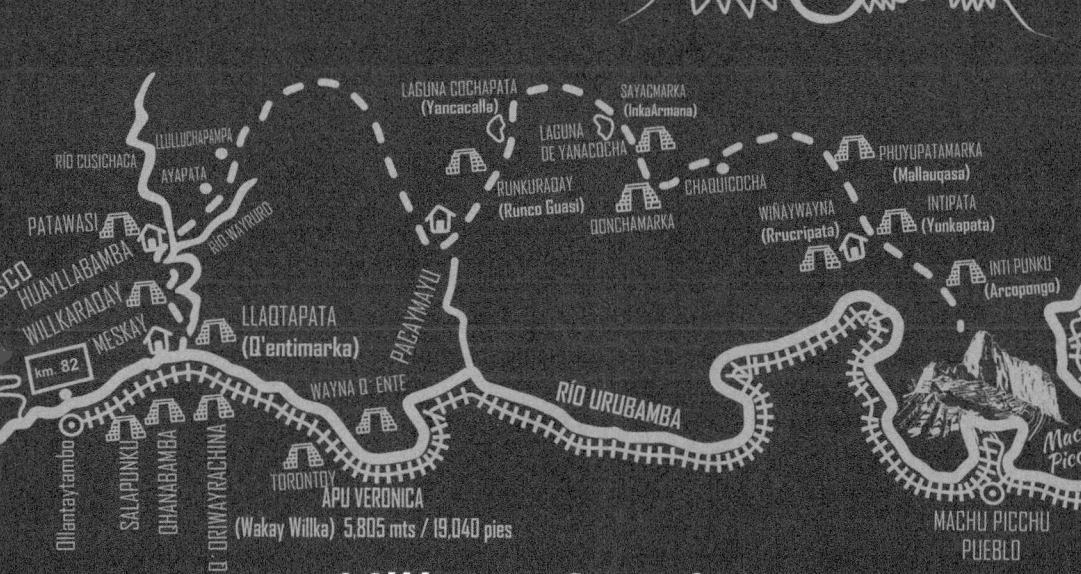

Hilbert Sumire

Dedicated to my mother and hero Teresa Bustincio Mendo, to
Thierry Jamin, who motivated me to write this book,
to my siblings Nickeil, Jenny, and Michel, to the people who
encouraged me Minoska Dávila, Adriana Flores,
Angela Ugarte, to my great friend Silverio Mendoza,
to my archaeologist friends and tour guides, such as
Ismael Uscachi, Oscar Montufar, Yolanda Sotelo,
Miguel Auccaylle.

To my Apus and to Pachamama.

THE INCA TRAIL TO MACHU PICCHU

INDEX

PREFACE 15
INTRODUCTION 23

PART ONE - THE INCAS OF CUSCO 29

CHAPTER I: THE CUSCO VALLEY BEFORE THE INCAS 31

The inhabitants of the Cusco Valley before the Spanish conquest 31
    Pre-ceramic period 32
    The Qhorqa Man 33
    The Chawaytiri Man 33
    The Canchis Man 33
    The Yauri Man 34
    The Chumbivilcas Man 34
    Cusco Formative Period 34
    The Formative Period, Phase "A", Marcavalle 36
    The Formative Period, Phase "B", Chanapata 37
    The regional states of the Cusco Valley 38
    The Qotakalli Regional State 39
    Killki Regional State 41
    The Regional State of Lucre 43
    Occupation and presence of the Waris in the Cusco valley. 44

CHAPTER II: ORIGIN OF THE INCA CULTURE IN THE CUSCO VALLEY 49
    The legend of Manco Capac and Mama Ocllo 49
    The legend of the Ayar brothers 52

CHAPTER III: THE INCAS BEFORE THE ARRIVAL OF THE SPANISH 57
    Mythical Incas 57
    Manco Capac 57

Sinchi Roca 59
Lloque Yupanqui 59
Mayta Capac 60
Capac Yupanqui 61
Inca Roca 62
Yahuar Huacac 64
Wiracocha 66
The historical Incas 70
CusiYupanqui (Pachacuteq) (1438 - 1471) 70
Inka Amaru Yupanqui 76
Tupac Inca Yupanqui (1471 - 1493) 77
Huayna Capac (1493 - 1527) 78
Huascar and Atahuallpa (1527 - 1533) 80

CHAPTER IV: THE RELIGION OF THE INCAS 83

Religion in the valley of Cusco before the Inca Pachacúteq 84
The religion of the Incas after the Inca Pachacuteq 87
Wiracocha, the Creator of the Universe 88
Inti, the Sun 89
Killa, the Moon 89
Chaska, the Star 90
Illapa, the Lightning 91
Kuychi, the Rainbow 91
Pachacamac, the god of Movement 92
Pachamama, Mother Earth 92
Apachetas 93
The apus, the sacred mountains 94
The huacas 95
The mallquis, the mummies 96

CHAPTER V: THE SOCIAL ORGANIZATION OF THE INCAS 99
    The Sapa Inca 100
    Nobility of blood 101
    The nobility of upstarts 102
    The people 103

PART TWO: THE INCA TRAIL TO MACHU PICCHU 105

CHAPTER VI: THE INCA ROADS 107
    The Qhapaq Ñan 108
    The Inca Trail to Machu Picchu and its regulation 111
    The Historic Sanctuary of Machu Picchu 111

CHAPTER VII: THE TRADITIONAL INCA TRAIL TO MACHU PICCHU (4 DAYS AND 3 NIGHTS) 117
    The Inca Trail to Machu Picchu 118
    Day 1 - Training day 121
    Salapunku 123
    Qhanabamba 127
    Wllkaraqay 130
    Llaqtapata (Q'entimarka) 133
    Patawasi 140
    Day 2 - The challenge 141
    Day 3: The adventure! 151
    Runkuraqay 155
    Sayacmarka 163
    Qonchamarka 168
    Phuyupatamarka 173
    Intipata 178
    Wiñaywayna 182
    Day 4 - Machu Picchu - We did it! 186

Inti Punku, the Sun gate 188
Recommendation before visiting the Inca citadel of Machu Picchu: 191

CHAPTER VIII: THE SHORT INCA TRAIL TO MACHU PICCHU (2 DAYS AND 1 NIGHT) 195

Day 1 - The adventure! 195
Chachabamba 196
Choquesuysuy 200
Day 2 - Let's explore the citadel of Machu Picchu 207
Recommendations before visiting Machu Picchu : 208

CHAPTER IX: MACHU PICCHU, INCA CITY 211

The search for Machu Picchu 214
Discovery Day 217
Let's visit the city of Machu Picchu 221
House of the Guardians 221
The agricultural sector 222
The Temple of the Three Gates 224
The Temple of the Sun 236
The House of the Inca 240
The Temple of Pachamama 241
The Quarry 243
The Temple of the Three Windows 246
The Main Temple 248
The Intiwatana 249
The Main Square 252
The Sacred Rock 253
The Huayna Picchu mountain 254
The urban sector 256
The Three Gates subsector 257

    The House of Morters 258

    The Temple of the Condor 259

CHAPTER X: BASIC INFORMATION FOR THE TRAIL TO MAKE THE INCA TRAIL TO MACHU PICCHU 261

    How is the Inca Trail program of 4 days and 3 nights? 261

    How is the Inca Trail program of 2 days and 1 night? 263

    How to book the Inca Trail 4 days and 3 nights? 263

    What does the tourist need to book the Inca Trail to Machu Picchu? 264

    How to book if the tourist wants to do the "short Inca trail" (2 days and 1 night) to Machu Picchu? 264

    What equipment is needed for the 4 days and 3 nights Inca Trail? 265

    What are the most common questions for the Inca Trail? 267

CHAPTER XI: STORIES OF THE INCA TRAIL 279

    Hold your llamas! 279

    A great challenge 284

    The biggest problem as a guide 288

BIBLIOGRAPHY 297

THE INCA TRAIL TO MACHU PICCHU

PREFACE
Incas fantastic stone roads

The famous Inca roads of the Qhapaq'Ñan were an enormous network of roads built during the Tawantinsuyu era that converged in the capital Cusco. Crossing the Andes and reaching altitudes of over five thousand meters, the roads linked the different regions of the Inca empire from north of the provincial capital of Quito to south of present-day Santiago, Chile. The road network covered approximately twenty-two thousand five hundred kilometers and provided access to an area of approximately three million square kilometers.

Today only a part of this road is visible. The rest has been destroyed by time and the construction of modern infrastructure. Between mountain ranges, high valleys, and deserts, the great Andean road is dotted with archaeological treasures and medium-sized sites in urgent need of protection.

This route crosses fifteen different ecosystems, four of which are endangered: the Peruvian Yungas, the dry forest of the Marañón, the rainforest, and the Chilean Matorral. The Qhapaq'Ñan also crosses many indigenous regions with fascinating but endangered cultures.

Several organizations, including UNESCO and the Peruvian Ministry of Culture, have begun working on these roads, emphasizing the urgency of their protection, in close collaboration with the governments of the six countries through which the Qhapaq'Ñan passes.

As the Incas did not use the wheel for transportation and did not have horses, the trails were only traveled by hikers, sometimes accompanied by pack animals, such as llamas. This road was the main economic and political integrating axis of the Inca Empire.

The central section was the main axis of the grandiose project of the Incas. It was a spinal column more than six thousand kilometers long. Its main route links the cities of Pasto in Colombia, Quito, and Cuenca in Ecuador, Cajamarca, and Cusco in Peru, Aconcagua in Argentina, and Santiago in Chile.

This road system consisted of two main north-south axes, one along the coast and the other in the mountains. There were other north-south axes and a secondary network of transversal roads linking the Andes with the Pacific coast and the Amazon basin.

At an altitude of between eight hundred and five thousand meters, this monumental road, which can be up to twenty meters wide, links inhabited areas, administrative centers, agricultural and mining areas, as well as places of worship. It allowed the Inca to control his empire and move his troops from Cusco. Most roads were paved with stones or cobblestones. In the desert, the road was marked with posts. As the road passed through mountainous areas, it became more tortuous and featured stairways and suspension bridges, made of ropes up to sixty meters long.

The state provided materials for road maintenance to ensure the passage of the army, high officials, but also the emperor and his messengers. The imperial messengers, or chasquis, took turns to ensure a rapid transfer. They could travel up to two hundred and forty kilometers in a single day. Villages near a bridge had to make sure it was maintained. But their inhabitants were fed by the state during construction.

When a major new road was built, it was named after the Sapa Inca who had it built. The government also built lodges, or tambos, along the Inca trails, separated by a day's walk. These also served as support posts for visiting state officials.

Cited by the first chroniclers of Peru, such as Francisco de Jérez or Pedro Sancho, secretaries of Francisco Pizarro, the Qhapaq'Ñan was a constant source of astonishing comments by all those who crossed the Andes during the colonial era. In 2014, the Qhapaq'Ñan was inscribed on the World Heritage of Humanity list.

During my extensive research, on the traces of Paititi, the lost city of the Incas, we have discovered large sections, not yet studied, of this immense road network. Located north of the department of Cusco, in the lost valleys of Lacco-Yavero or Chunchusmayo, these stone paths are bordered by magnificent Inca or pre-Inca sites. Some of them border the Andean peaks at more than five thousand meters in a northerly direction. Others get lost further east in the heart of the Amazon jungle, in this still unexplored Antisuyu. But how far do they go? It remains a mystery.

I congratulate my friend Hilbert Sumire, member of the Inkarri Institute, and director of our research projects, for having dared to undertake the writing of this book dedicated to the magnificent Inca trail that led travelers from Cusco in ancient times to Machu Picchu. Even today, the "globetrotters" of the 21st century continue to travel these same stone paths, with breathtaking panoramas !

No one was better qualified than Hilbert to write this guide, which will be an indispensable tool for discovering the secrets of the ancient archaeological sites that have been known for centuries on this "sacred route".

Cusco, this Sunday, April 10th, 2021

Thierry Jamin

THE INCA TRAIL TO MACHU PICCHU

Map of the Qhapaq Ñan.

Map of Peru. Location of Cusco.

THE INCA TRAIL TO MACHU PICCHU

INTRODUCTION

I was born in the city of Cusco. Since I was a child, I felt very fond of the history of the Incas, for the greatness of this great culture that developed throughout the Andes Mountains, being the city of Cusco, the capital of the Inca State.

After finishing my secondary studies in the Great School Unit "Inca Garcilaso de la Vega", I studied the technical career of Official Tourist Guide, in the Superior Technological Institute "Tupac Amaru" in the city of Cusco, where I was born the passion for walking in the mountains, doing my work as a mountain guide for more than 25 years. I have walked the different treks in the Cusco area and especially the famous Inca Trail to the city of Machu Picchu more than 775 times.

I studied at the Universidad Nacional San Antonio Abad del Cusco (UNSAAC), obtaining in 2006 the degree of Bachelor in Archaeology with the thesis "*Archaeological Prospecting in the Apu Mama Coltama, Ocrobamba Community, District of Mariscal Gamarra, Province of Grau, Department of Apurimac*".

As an archaeologist, I carried out different archaeological works in the area of Cusco and other cities. In April 2012, I was Director of Archaeological Research in the Inca citadel of Machu Picchu with the "*Surface Archaeological Research Project (without *excavation) in the Inca city of Machu Picchu"*, finding in this research a funerary context, possibly of high rank.

In 2016, I was part of the "Inkarri Cusco" Institute prestigious institution. As an active member of this organization, I participate in discovering the famous mythical city of the Incas: "El Paititi" (or El Dorado).

As an archaeologist, I continue to carry out archaeological exploration, monitoring, and archaeological research. And a personal challenge, as well as the group I belong to, "Inkarri Cusco", is to discover the mythical city of Paititi.

As a Mountain Guide, I continue to do the different treks in the Cusco area and surrounding places, especially the Inca Trail to Machu Picchu. Being in the mountains is to be in contact with Mother Nature. From her, I learned and keep on learning respect and love for her.

This book tries to explain and understand the origin of the Inca culture in the Cusco valley. It also tries to support the Inca trail to the city of Machu Picchu as a place of pilgrimage, since it has several ceremonial centers along the way. It also provides some important recommendations for the sacred route to the wonder of the world.

The book is divided into two parts: in the first part, it tries to explain the first human occupations, located in the high parts of the mountains or punas, inhabited by groups of humans who were dedicated to the domestication and grazing of camelids, llamas and alpacas. Later, these human groups began to occupy the valleys in search of better lands, discovering agriculture and settling in a territory, beginning to build houses, ceremonial places, and at the time of carrying out the activity of trade, beginning the construction of roads that allow them to communicate from one valley to another.

INTRODUCTION

The appearance of the first human settlements follows an evolutionary and developmental sequence in the Cusco Valley in a historical process from the Pre- ceramic, Formative Period, Regional States, the Wari occupation in the Cusco Valley, and finally the establishment of the great Inca State.

All these explanations are given through their legends that have passed down from generation to generation in the Peruvian people, from their first Inca, or ruler, until the arrival of the Spanish to the Inca territory, where a bloody civil war occurred between the brothers Huascar and Atahualpa with the consequent conquest of the Inca people by the Spanish.

The Inca religion from the first sovereign, Manco Capac, was governed by the social class of the *Hurin*. And from Pachacuteq begins a new religious system governed by the *Hanan*, being the Sun, the supreme god. The Inca began to be considered as the son of the sun. All this added to a social organization, where the *ayllu* or family was the base.

The second part deals with the Inca road network before the arrival of the Spaniards, which was used during the Colonial and Republican periods and is still used today by the inhabitants of the Andes.

The Inca Trail to Machu Picchu, is the most famous road in South America, the same that today is protected and preserved by the Peruvian government and subject to strict regulations. This road has in its journey, from the starting point to reach the city of Machu Picchu, a large number of Inca complexes, of which are villages, ceremonial centers, resting places, agricultural complexes, deposits, control places, altars, and at the end of this walk you reach this place of pilgrimage called Machu Picchu.

The Inca city of Machu Picchu, since it was discovered, has kept a great enigma that to this day continues to be studied by local archaeologists from Cusco, Peru and the world, remaining an open book to many investigations and questions.

At the end of this book, as a mountain guide, with more than 25 years of having traveled this "sacred route", I want to give you some recommendations on how to do this great hike.

Now, I invite you to explore and discover this fantastic Inca trail to the magical city of Machu Picchu.

THE INCA TRAIL TO MACHU PICCHU

PART ONE
THE INCAS OF CUSCO

CHAPTER I
THE CUSCO VALLEY BEFORE THE INCAS

Talking about the Incas is a fascinating subject for study and debate. It would take us to read too many books and in the end, we would be left with many questions. This was a civilization or culture very specific to the Andes Mountains, very different from the cultures that developed in Europe or other parts of the world.

To understand what the Inca culture was, it has to be analyzed before the arrival of the Spaniards to the South American continent.

The inhabitants of the Cusco Valley before the Spanish conquest

According to the studies carried out by one of the pioneers of archaeology in the Cusco area, Dr. Luis Barreda Murillo, a native of Puno, but from Cusco at heart. In his work *"History and Pre Inca Archaeology"*, of the Institute of Andean Archaeology Machu Picchu (1995), he carried out an arduous task of investigation in the area of Cusco and surrounding places, to understand the origin and beginning of this culture that developed in the current imperial valley. This for an understanding at the local and regional levels.

The author considers the following periods: the pre-ceramic period, the formative or ayllus period, the period of the regional states, and the period of the Great Inca State.

Pre-ceramic period

The pre-ceramic period is the time before the discovery of the pottery of the inhabitants of the Cusco valley.

They are the inhabitants living in the high Andean zones, living in caves or shelters. They are dedicated to the domestication of South American camelids such as the *llama*, the *alpaca*, and the domestication of the *guinea pig* in a primitive way, in flat places where there is enough presence of ichu, or straw, and other local plants that will constitute the main food of these animals. It is a grazing stage, but at the same time, the domestication process of other agricultural products such as potatoes, *añu*, *oca*, *olluco*, *qui-*

Mural fresco by Juan Bravo. Detail, pre-ceramic period, Cusco, June 1992.

noa, and *kañigua,* very typical products of this ecological zone, is taking place.

It is a stage of beginning agriculture. It is the settler who in his shelter or cave will represent his daily life through rock painting, with scenes of hunting and herding of camelids, making projectile points or weapons made of lithic fragments of flint, basalt, jasper, and quartz.

To this period belong the "Qhorqa Man", the "Chawaytiri Man", the "Canchis Man", the "Yauri Man" and the "Chumbivilcas Man".

The Qhorqa Man

The Qhorqa Man is located in the district of Qhorqa, province of Cusco, Cusco region, in the sector called Torre Q'aqa. Its archaeological evidence is found in caves or rock shelters with rock paintings depicting scenes of camelid herding.

The Chawaytiri Man

The Chawaytiri Man is located in the former hacienda, today a cooperative for raising camelids, cattle, and sheep, between the areas of Pisac and Paucartambo. Its archaeological evidence is in caves, with the presence of cave paintings, which show scenes of camelid herding.

The Canchis Man

The Canchis Man is located in the provinces of Canchis, in the districts of Sicuani, Marangani, San Pedro, San Pablo, Combapata, Pitumarka, and Checacupe. Its archaeological evidence is in caves, with the presence of camelid cave paintings, in white color. The interesting thing about the Man of Canchis is that there is still the presence of very large *canchon* constructions, giving evidence that this man already had the work of raising and grazing llamas and alpacas, as well as the construction of traps for wild camelids, possibly *guanacos* and *vicuñas*. Lithic instruments such as scrapers, flint projectile points, and quartz knives were found in their caves, showing a knowledge of the manufacture of weapons and/or tools.

The Yauri Man

The Yauri Man is located in the province of Espinar, in flat places, of great territorial extension for the breeding and grazing of camelids. It covers other territories of Arequipa such as Cotahuasi, Caylloma, Chivay, where there are pre-ceramic remains. In its caves and shelters, there are cave paintings with scenes of hunting and camelid breeding, with red, black, brown, and white colors, associated with lithic instruments and flint projectile points. Near its caves, in the same way, there is the presence of **canchones** made of carved stones.

The Chumbivilcas Man

The Chumbivilcas Man is located in the Eponima province of the department of Cusco. Evidence has also been found in other places such as Qhapaqmarka, Ch'amaca, Livitaca, Kiñota, and Velille. Its archaeological evidence is in caves, with cave paintings, associated with lithic instruments of basalt and slate stone or projectile points.

Cusco Formative Period

This Formative period is characterized by the migration of the high Andean settlers to the valleys, where they find better climatic and living conditions. That is to say, to be able to dedicate themselves to the work of agriculture, mainly the cultivation of corn, potatoes, and other agricultural products. They began a process of "sedentarization", that is, to establish themselves in

CHAPTER I: THE CUSCO VALLEY BEFORE THE INCAS

a certain geographical location, to coexist with their ecological environment, to begin to build a place to live, to establish family kinship ties, or ayllu. The ayllu was the basis of an economic, political, and religious organization. They also began to build small human settlements, in a territorial area, especially in the ancient valley of Huatanay (Cusco city), with a chronology of 1,000 years B.C. They will become a group of corn and potato farmers, developing an irrigation system, construction of cultivation platforms on slopes, or cultivation terraces.

These first human settlements were called Marcavalle and Chanapata, which covered from the area of Santa Ana to the valley of Angostura. Local archaeologists have denominated them as Formative Period Phase "A", Marcavalle; and Formative Period Phase "B", Chanapata. Each with its characteristics in terms of ceramics, architecture, and social organization.

Mural fresco by Juan Bravo. Detail, Formative period, Cusco, June 1992.

The Formative Period, Phase "A", Marcavalle

The archaeological site of Marcavalle is located in the current neighborhood of journalists, next to the *Institute of Minors of Marcavalle*, in the city of Cusco. In 1954, Professor Manuel Chávez Ballón, together with the students of the professional career of Anthropology of the UNSAAC, Cusco, and with the collaboration of the North American researcher Patricia Lyon, discovered ceramic fragments in the site called Marcavalle. Thanks to these findings, they were able to determine the presence of their cultural occupation, with a thick stratum, without mixing with another cultural settlement. In other words, the inhabitants of the Cusco valley, pre-Inca, and Inca respected the site as the beginning and origin of this Andean culture.

The Phase A period, Marcavalle, has an antiquity of 1,000 years B.C., until 700 years B.C., occupying a great territorial area in the territories of the valley of Cusco, and including other places such as the provinces of Anta, Paruro, Canchis, Quispicanchis, Urubamba and Chumbivilcas.

In the excavations carried out at the Marcavalle site, ceramic fragments have been found, predominantly black, as well as brown and red, in the form of pots with two handles, small "cantaros", flat base plates, with geometric, zoomorphic (felines), anthropomorphic and combined, ceremonial ceramics with decorations.

In terms of architecture, they are adobe or mud constructions joined with mud mortar, rectangular, or circular with roofs. They are made of sticks of local trees, *queuña, alder, chachacomo,* and *straw*. They must have their ceremonial centers.

CHAPTER I: THE CUSCO VALLEY BEFORE THE INCAS

The Formative Period, Phase "B", Chanapata

In 1941, the North American archaeologist Dr. Jhon R. Rowe, discovered in the area of the Saphy ravine and the Carmenca hill, belonging to the parish of Santa Ana, fragments of Inca ceramics already known. Then, far below, he found a new type of ceramic, for which he denominated it Chanapata, giving it an antiquity of 800 years B.C., up to 1,000 years. A.D. Dr. Rowe found domestic and ceremonial ceramics with a better firing, with thick edges. The pottery is decorated.

As for its architecture, in the areas of Wimpillay and Santa Ana, in the Saphy ravine, its constructions are conical in shape, built with sandstone and boulders joined by a mud mortar, with the possible use of adobes. The stones were possibly extracted from the Saphy River.

For Dr. Luis Barreda Murillo, for the characteristics of the ceramics and the motifs of decoration, the Chanapata would be the heirs or direct descendants of the technology of the Marcavalles. The use of lands can be the same since in many places of Marcavalle occupation there is a cultural presence of the Chanapata.

Chanapata pottery is widespread throughout the Cusco valley such as Wimpillay, Picchu, Muyo Orqo, Granja Kayra, as well as places outside the Cusco valley such as Quispicanchis, Canchis, Paruro, Calca, Acomayo, and Anta, covering a large territorial area, i.e. the Cusco valley and the Anta pampas.

The Chanapatas, like the Marcavalles, would have been the pioneers of the social organization based on the ayllu, from a gerontocratic government, based on an economy of reciprocity such as the Ayni and Minka, dynamizing the commercial system of products called *challay*, or barter, as well as reciprocity with their gods.

In the place called Chanapata, during the excavations made by Jhon H. Rowe, terraces were found, which would be the oldest or earliest, for agricultural purposes. The construction techniques are very simple. The importance would be how the man of Chanapata modifies the natural landscape to create cultivation lands, which have been widely used by the Incas throughout their territorial domain.

Phase "A", or Marcavalle, and Phase "B", or Chanapata, would be the oldest cultural human settlements in the Cusco valley.

The regional states of the Cusco Valley

With the establishment of the Marcavalles and Chanapatas in the Cusco valley, the ayllu was the basis of the economic, political, social, and religious organizations.

Mural fresco by Juan Bravo. Detail, the period of the regional States, Cusco, June 1992.

CHAPTER I: THE CUSCO VALLEY BEFORE THE INCAS

There is the development of an agricultural system, with corn and potato crops as the main food. Grazing and raising camelids (llamas and alpacas), building places to live (houses), while establishing a village with a larger territorial area, to begin to make their pottery with their technology, with decorations, designs of geometric shapes, zoomorphic and anthropomorphic. Elements that already provide the idea of a mode of religion in the Cusco valley.

They are the Marcavalles and Chanapatas, who will appoint a chief or *kuraq, the* oldest of the families, to govern and control the human group from the political, economic, social, and religious aspects. These ayllus would confront each other and the winner would assume control of the ayllus and their territories, constituting the first regional state in the valley of Cusco.

The Qotakalli Regional State

Dr. Manuel Chávez Ballón was the first archaeologist to find this new type of pottery in the Cusco valley, located in the sector occupied by the Joven Araway people, south of the city of Cusco, where the Peruvian coat of arms is engraved.

In 1964, Dr. Luis Barreda Murillo found in the archaeological complex of Pikillaqta fragments of pottery decorated as well-fired clay bowls, with cream-colored paste, with black, red, and cream-colored decorations.

Subsequently, archaeological excavations were carried out in Qotakalli and Wimpillay, where evidence of ceramics from the Qotakalli regional state was found. It was dated between 400 - 500 A.D., that is, before the invasion of the Waris in the valley of Cusco. And it was the Qotakallis who initiated the process of expulsion of the Waris from the Cusco valley, knowing that this invasion probably took place in 750 AD.

The Qotakallis would probably be contemporary and a little later than the Waris, and the indirect ancestors of Lucre and Killki. This state would have lasted about 600 years.

As for their ceramics, the Qotakallis would have inherited from their ancestors, the Marcavalles and Chanapatas, the technology and manufacture of the same, but with improved or advanced technology in terms of firing, clay quality, design, and especially the polychrome decoration (various colors), such as red, black and light cream. Its forms were bowls, pitchers, plates, cups, and pots. But at the same time, it presents an influence of the Waris who arrived in the valley of Cusco approximately 750 AD. Their influence is given in the forms and decoration that are the tripoid and polychrome vessels.

In the Araway and Tankarpata areas of Cusco, more than eighty enclosures or dwellings have been identified, built with edged stones, joined with mud mortar, with a rectangular floor plan of 9 meters long, 5 meters wide and 1.5 meters high, roofed with sticks from local trees and thatch. Knowing terms of housing construction and the use of a simple architecture.

The expansion of the Qotakallis would cover a large area, passing the limits of the Cusco valley, such as the areas of the Vilcanota valley -the Sacred Valley of the Incas-, Calca, San Salvador, Paruro, Urcos, Sicuani, San Pedro. This would mean the presence of settlers in different ecological levels such as the *puna*, *qheswa*, and *yunka*. They exchanged agricultural products utilizing the *challay* of potato, corn, coca leaves, and other agricultural products. Salt was a very important product for the conservation of llama and alpaca meat, or *charki*. Also natural resources for the construction of houses such as straw sticks from trees, clay for the manufacture of ceramics. Everything is linked to the construction of roads, for the communication of the settlers from one valley to another, and the llamas used for the transport of agricultural products through trade.

It is important to mention, in this stage of the regional development of the Qotakallis, the invasion of the Waris will take place in the valley of Cusco, around 750 AD. It would be up to the Qotakallis, Killkis, and Lucres to confront them.

The Waris, after defeating the Qotakallis, settled in the southern part of the Cusco valley, influencing ceramics, architecture, sculpture, and, why not, religious, political, and social, probably until 1,000 AD.

When the Qotakallis disappeared from the Cusco valley, they would be succeeded by the Killki regional state, who would occupy the same places as the Qotakallis. The Qotakallis would leave their inheritance in terms of economic, political, and social organization, based on the great system of the ayllu, which would be the basis for the development of agriculture and camelid grazing. The regional state of Qotakalli would be the ancestors of the *Killki* people.

Killki Regional State

The Killki regional state is located in the Cusco valley, on the right bank of the Watanay River, in front of the San Sebastian district, in the sector known today as Pillaw.

In 1943, Dr. Jhon H. Rowe, in the archaeological excavations carried out in Q'oricancha, in the sector called the Canchón, found a style of pottery very different from that of the Incas, baptizing the ceramic style as Killki, which means "canchón". He dated it to between 800 and 1,100 A.D.

As for ceramics, the Killkis will continue to use the same clay mines as the Qotakallis. But as for the manufacture of the same ones, there is a technological advance especially in the binder, which allows a better firing and a greater duration of the ceramic. For decoration they use light and dark red, white, brown, and black colors, with geometric, anthropomorphic, and zoomorphic motifs, maintaining a Qotakalli style. Their pottery is found in the places occupied by the Lucre and Incas. They also left evidence of an influence of elements of the Waris, with whom they shared time and territorial space in the Cusco valley.

The Killkis expanded their territorial area, occupying the Vilcanota Valley, Calca, Urubamba, Ollantaytambo, Anta, Acomayo, Paucartambo, Paruro, Quispicanchis, Canchis, and the valley of La Convención, in the province of Quillabamba. In agriculture, they will dominate several ecological levels, intensively cultivating corn, potatoes, *olluco, mashwa, oqa, tarwi,* and *quinoa*. In the yunka or jungle, they will cultivate *coca* leaf, *yuka, sweet potato,* and *unkucha*. And in the high parts of the *puna*, such as in Cusco, Calca, Urubamba, Paruro, Quispicanchis, and Canchis, they would devote themselves to grazing and raising camelids, such as llamas and alpacas.

In terms of architecture, evidence has been found in different places, especially in their occupied areas from the Cusco valley, Vilcanota valley, La Convención area, and high parts of the puna. As temples and enclosures, or dwellings, built with edged stones, carved andesite, and other stones, joined with clay mortar. Such as those found in the Q'oricancha of Cusco, current temple of Santo Domingo, Wimpillay, Chincheros and Ollantaytambo.

The social organization of the Killkis, like their ancestors the Qotakallis, would have been based on the ayllu system, which would have been scattered throughout their area of occupation, governed by the oldest person in the ayllu, that is, a gerontocratic government.

Their religion would be based on the worship of their gods, such as *Choquechinchay, Qoa* or *Titi* (puma), *Kuntur* (the condor), and *Illapa* (Lightning). The serpent would represent the water element. Finally, condor, puma, and snake symbolize the famous *Andean trilogy.*

The exchange between the regional states of the Killkis and Lucres, and their alliance, allowed the expulsion of the *Wari* invaders from the Cusco valley, around 1,100 A.D., to give rise to the great Inca culture or state.

The Regional State of Lucre

The regional state of Lucre, possibly appeared in the valley of Cusco in the year 800 A.D., to then become a regional state. Its possible location would be in the district of Lucre, in the sector called Choquepugyu, very close to the archaeological complex of Pikillaqta, a settlement of the Wari culture.

In the archaeological works carried out in Choquepugyu, ceramics inherited from the Killkis have been found. However, there is an improvement in terms of technology, improvement of the binder (clay, sand, and a lot of mica), for a better firing of ceramics, better-firing kilns, manufacture of larger vessels such as arībalos, to store agricultural products and seeds such as *corn*, quinoa, *kañiwa*, salt, and others.

The Lucre ceramics are decorated with geometric, anthropomorphic, and zoomorphic motifs of the local fauna (felines, birds, and camelids), as well as anthropomorphic representations of human faces. The colors used were white, cream, red, black, and brown. There are two types of ceramics: Lucre A ceramics, a direct descendant of the Killki ceramics, and Lucre B ceramics, influenced by Wari ceramics.

In terms of architecture, the Lucres used building materials such as stone (sandstone, limestone, diorite, and andesite edged and polished) and adobe, bonded with mud mortar. The roofing of the enclosures, houses, and temples, has been the same as their ancestors the Killkis, sticks of local trees, covered with thatch, which would have reached a height of 7 meters, such as those existing in the archaeological complex of Choquepugyu.

The Lucres would continue with the same tradition of the Killkis of reusing the sites to rebuild some temples or ceremonial places, such as the findings in the Qoricancha, using green diorite. The area of expansion of the Lucres is in all the provinces of the department of Cusco, such as Calca, Urubamba, La Convención, Paruro, Paucartambo, Acomayo, Quispicanchis, Chumbivilcas, Canchis, Canas and controlling the entire Cusco valley.

The Lucres will build roads, bridges, cultivation terraces, and a system of water channels to improve their agricultural system. Having a technological advance, a mastery of the ecological levels that will be the basis of their economy, political and social.

With the presence of the Waris in the valley of Cusco, it gave origin to the union of both regional States the Killkis and Lucres, to confederate, to form a "common state", to confront and expel the Waris of the valley of Cusco, giving origin to the creation of the great Inca State. Their rulers succeeded one another until the appearance of the great Inca ruler Pachacuteq, in the middle of the year 1420 AD. Who would make great changes in the economic, political, social, and religious aspects, who would also begin to expand the Inca territory to other territories?

Occupation and presence of the Waris in the Cusco valley.

The occupation and presence of the Waris in the valley of Cusco is given in the year 750 AD. This is based on the archaeological findings of the North American Dr. Jhon H. Rowe, made in the Cusco valley in 1956.

CHAPTER I: THE CUSCO VALLEY BEFORE THE INCAS

One evidence that can be seen today is found towards the south of the Cusco valley, on the slopes of the Huchuy Balcon hill: the so-called pre-Inca archaeological complex called Pikillaqta.

Pikillaqta has been studied by travelers and researchers such as George Squier in the mid-nineteenth century, the Cusquenian historian Luis E. Valcárcel (1930), Jhon Rowe and Luis Barreda Murillo.

The Wari culture developed in the department of Ayacucho. It began around 100 BC. Like all cultures in their process of territorial expansion, the Waris soon arrived in the Cusco valley. Their occupation would be for an estimated time between 540 and 900 A.D., occupation evaluated thanks to the archaeological complex of Pikillaqta: more than 350 years of occupation.

The urban complex of Pikillaqta is composed of a walled area 1 kilometer long by 800 meters wide, with more than 700 enclosures between houses, with one floor and two floors to the residence sector (500 approximately) and deposits, or *qollqas*, for the storage of products, of quadrangular plant, with large courts, delimiting spaces with a respective access opening, without the presence of windows. Some buildings have niches or false windows, in rectangular shape. The construction materials used would be sandstone edged with mud mortar. Some have plaster stuccoes.

There is a gypsum mine, very close to this archaeological complex. The interior is white. The roofs would be made of alder, queuña, chachacomo, and thatched roofs.

However, the studies carried out by Dr. Luis Barreda Murillo and the North American archaeologist Gordon Mc. Ewan, provide us with more precise data on who built Pikillaqta: large buildings, thatched roofs, water transportation system through canals and aqueducts such as those of Rumiqollqa, which were reused and modified by the great Inca State.

In addition to Pikillaqta, there are other places of Wari occupation, such as the Rumiqollqa water canal. This canal is very close to the Batan Orqo and Qotoqotuyoq warrior complexes, near the towns of Urcos, in the Cusco valley, in the Wimpillay sector and other provinces such as Acomayo, Paruro, Canchis, Chumbivilcas, and Espinar.

The occupation of the Waris in the Cusco valley is presumed to have been peaceful on their route from Ayacucho to Cusco, passing through the provinces of Paruro, Chumbivilcas, and Espinar. Their presence was from 540 to 900 years AD.

The expulsion of the Waris from the Cusco valley would end with a violent expulsion through wars caused by the alliance of the Killkis and Lucres, to give way to the origin of the Inca culture.

CHAPTER I: THE CUSCO VALLEY BEFORE THE INCAS

PERIODIFICATION OF THE ANDEAN CULTURE OF CUSCO

PERIODS	HUMAN SETTLEMENTS		CHRONOLOGY
INKA STATE	3rd PHASE INKA INVASION ANS SPANISH ETNOCIDO		1,532 A.D..
	2nd PHASE INKA EXPANSIVE		1,400 A.D..
	1st INITIAL PHASE		1,110 A.D..
REGIONAL STATES	LUCRE KILLKI	INVASION WARI 750 D.C.	1,000 A.D. 800 A.D..
	QOTAKALLI		600 A.D..
FORMATIVE	2da PHASE CHANAPATA		800 A.D.
	1ra PHASE MARCAVALLE		1,000 A.D..
PRE-CERAMICO	AGRICULTURE SHEPHERD COLLECTORS	MAN OF: QORQA CHAWAYTIRI CANCHIS CHUMBIVILVAS YAURI	5,000 A.D..

INSTITUTE OF ANDEAN ARCHITECTURE MACHUPICCHU
Dr. Luis Barreda M. Cuzco - 1994

PERIOD OF THE PRE-HISPANIC SOCIAL EVOLUTION OF CUZCO	
INKA STATE	1,100 A.D..
REGIONAL STATE	600 A.D..
FORMATIVE	1,000 A.D..
PRE-CERAMICO	5,000 A.D..

INSTITUTE OF ANDEAN ARCHITECTURE MACHUPICCHU
Dr. Luis Barreda M. Cuzco - 1994[1]

---

[1] Luis Barreda Murillo, "Historia y Arqueologia del Qosqo Pre-Inka", pag. 88-89, Cusco, 1995.

THE INCA TRAIL TO MACHU PICCHU

CHAPTER II
ORIGIN OF THE INCA CULTURE IN THE CUSCO VALLEY

All ancient civilizations in the world have created myths and legends about their origin. A clear example of the Roman culture is the legend of the creation of the great Roman empire by the brothers Remus and Romulus. Other examples are the cultures of Mesoamerica, with the Maya and the Aztecs, about their highest deity, the god *Quetzalqoal*, or *Kukulcan*. For the South American culture, i.e. the Incas, we also find myths and legends to explain their origin.

In the Inca culture, we have two very traditional legends, which we have been taught since elementary school until today: the "legend of Manco Capac and Mama Ocllo" and the "legend of the Ayar brothers".

The legend of Manco Capac and Mama Ocllo

The mestizo chronicler[2], Inca Garcilaso de la Vega[3], in his famous chronicle *"Comentarios Reales de los Incas"* (1609), mentions the mythical origin of the foundation of the Inca empire. The legend says:

> *"In lands near Lake Titicaca, there were uncivilized human beings, who had no religion, justice, culture, social organization, knowledge of agriculture.*
>
> *"The Sun God (Inti), felt pity and decided to civilize these men and women. He asked his beloved children Manco Capac and Mama Ocllo, who would be Manco Capac's sister and wife, to descend upon the earth and build a great empire. Manco Capac and Mama*

---

[2] His father was Spanish, Sebastián Garcilaso de la Vega Vargas and his mother was Inca, Isabel Chimpu Ocllo.
[3] 1539 - 1616.

Ocllo, took the message of their father the Sun God, with much joy to teach men, to live in a civilized way and to venerate their creator God the Sun.

"Manco Capac and Mama Ocllo were to found the capital of the Empire of the Sun and a city of gold. Therefore, the Sun God gave them a gold stick and said to them:

- Manco Capac, Mama Ocllo, my children, you are going to leave this great Lake Titicaca and go in a northerly direction. But in every place, that you rest to eat or sleep, gently hit the ground, with the golden stick that I gave you, and in that place where this golden stick sinks, there you will build the great empire, which will be the capital of this great empire of the Sun.

"The next day, they set out among the foaming waters of Lake Titicaca. They began their march very slowly across the surface of the crystalline waters, a sacred place for the rising of the

Monument by Juan Bravo. Detail, Manco Capac and Mama Ocllo, Limacpampa square, Cusco.

CHAPTER II: ORIGIN OF THE INCA CULTURE IN THE CUSCO VALLEY

children of the Sun. The uncivilized men saw them and knew the brightness of their clothes and their gold jewelry. They were afraid at the sight of the Inca and bowed their heads. They understood that they were gods, who followed them on their journey hidden among the rocks and bushes.

"Manco Capac and Mama Ocllo marched northward as their father, the Sun God, had instructed them. Days and nights passed. They rested and ate, trying to sink the golden stick. Finally, one day, they came to a beautiful place. It was a valley with imposing hills. They rested and tried again to sink the gold stick. This time, very slowly, it sank. They were at the Wanacauri hill. They had reached the right place and saw from the top of the hill a beautiful valley: it was the Cusco valley.

Manco Capac told the men who had followed them:

- I am the son of the Sun. We have to worship him, teaching them to cultivate the land, to hunt, to build canals and their houses.

"The men knelt, and Mama Ocllo taught the women how to use the distaff, to weave the wool of the llama, alpaca, and vicuña. He taught them how to make their clothes. He taught them how to cook and dedicate themselves to the household, learning from the men and women."

Manco Capac would become the first conqueror who established the first ayllus. He conquered 7 to 9 new leagues around the Cusco valley, such as Paucartambo, Limatambo Pakarectampu. He is credited with the first dual division. Those who descend through the paternal line are the *Hanan Qosqo*. Those of the coya, the official wife of the Inca, on the female side, will be the *Hurin Qosqo*.

Manco Capac will be the first Inca, or ruler, the first organizer of this future great empire that developed and expanded throughout the Andes.

The legend of the Ayar brothers

This legend was collected by the mestizo chronicler Guaman Poma de Ayala (1600), and the Spanish chroniclers Cieza de León (1553) and Juan de Betanzos (1551). Let's listen to the legend:

"Many years ago, in a place called Tamputoqo hill of Pakareqtampu, there were three holes. One morning, the sun shone into those holes. It was illuminated and four men and four women came out of it. They were Manco Capac and his wife Mama Ocllo, Ayar Auca and his wife Mama Rahua, Ayar Cachi, and Mama Qora, and finally Ayar Cachi and Mama Huaco.

Mural fresco by Juan Bravo. Detail, the legend of the Ayar brothers, Cusco, June 1992.

CHAPTER II: ORIGIN OF THE INCA CULTURE IN THE CUSCO VALLEY

"The god Teqsi Wiracocha, the creator of the universe, gave them the task of searching for new and fertile lands where they had to cultivate the most precious product, which was corn, which the god wanted to share with other human beings.

"Each one of them had special powers to fulfill this task. Mama Huaco, was a beautiful woman, warrior, and strong. Ayar Cachi was the strongest of them all. It is said that when Ayar Cachi got angry, he would throw stones with his sling and turn the mountains into valleys. Ayar Uchú was mystical and religious. His wife, Mama Qora, was the one who transmitted the secrets of medicinal plants. Ayar Auca was the right arm of Manco Capac. Mama Rahua was a homely and talented woman. She could play music and weave textiles. Ayar Manco was cunning and intelligent. He brought with him a falcon named Inti. Mama Ocllo was beautiful, in charge of preserving seeds.

" The god Tecqsi Wiracocha gave Manco Capac a golden barrel, that he would sink the same in every place he would arrive, to locate fertile lands where they would stay. Mama Huaco, was the leader. She was the strongest. She told her brothers:

- Let's look for fertile land!

"So they came to the lands of Hahuanacancha, where they lived for a while. Mama Ocllo brought seeds from Tambuputoqo. But these lands were not very fertile and they decided to move forward, reaching the lands of Pallata and Tampukiro, without good results, on that journey. Ayar Cachi, with his sling, throwing stones, turned the hills into valleys.

Fearful, Ayar Cachi's brothers, with deceit, told him to return to Tambutoqo to bring the map or insignia of power and some golden vessels and corn seeds. Ayar Cachi, at first, did not want to go.

"But Mama Huaco rebuked him:

- How can you be such a coward! If you are the strongest among all the brothers.

"Ashamed, he returned. Ayar Cachi returned to Tambutoqo. A faithful servant of the Ayar brothers, named Tambuchay, accompanied him. When Ayar Cachi entered the cave of Tambutoqo, he closed the cave with blocks of stone. Ayar, being in the cave, made the mountain rumble, turning Tambuchay into a block of stone that exists to this day. When he managed to get out of the cave, he became a bird with large wings. He forgave his brothers. The brothers began to cry. With much pain, they arrived at Qirimanta.

"Here the brothers were organized. Ayar Manco would be the leader. Ayar Uchú would be in charge of the religious part and Ayar Auca would be in charge of taking over the new lands. When they arrived at Cerro Wanacauri and as they walked, they saw a bright rainbow in the distance, which was a sign of a good sign. They climbed the mountain. From where they saw the beginning of the rainbow they saw a rock that was a Huaca. Ayar Uchú jumped on the Huaca. And as he sat down, he turned to stone. The brothers ran to him.

"Ayar Uchu, turning to stone said to them:

- Just remember me!

"Ayar Manco promised to remember him in his ceremonies. The Ayar brothers continued on their way. They arrived at a place called Matahua where they built their huts, cultivated corn, where they stayed for two years. Mama Huaco, one day, threw two spears: one to Collpa Pampa, which was loose land, and the other to the lands of Huaynapata, which was more fertile land.

"The brothers returned to the area of Matahua. Ayar Manco, from this place, saw a large rock in the distance, sending his brother Ayar Auca, who sprouted large wings. Arriving at this great rock, Ayar Manco and the women followed him, where they met local settlers, whom they confronted.

CHAPTER II: ORIGIN OF THE INCA CULTURE IN THE CUSCO VALLEY

Ayar Manco and Mama Huaco faced each other. Mama Huaco, with great ferocity, killed and pulled out of one of them his heart. Seeing this, the other villagers escaped. Ayar Manco ordered to build on this great rock the temple to the god Inti, which he called the Inticancha or the House of the Sun. Being this the first ceremonial place, and its surroundings, he ordered to build many terraces, thus beginning a process of expansion to neighboring towns. Being at the same time the first conqueror of the Cusco valley and its surroundings, thus becoming the first Inca and founder of the great empire of the Incas".

According to Maria Rostorowsky, a great scholar of Inca culture, the legend of Manco Capac and Mama Ocllo is something mythical. According to her, it would be a beautiful story. However, this story would be a pure invention of the Inca chronicler Garcilaso de la Vega. For other researchers, it sounds more like the creation of the world given by the Catholic religion compared to Adam and Eve, the first parents of humanity. For Rostorowsky, the legend of the Ayar brothers has more historical support, proof of which are the constructions in the area of Pakareqtampu.

Both legends, real or not, credible or not, will be the source of information to explain the origin of the Incas in the Cusco valley; and thus begin their process of expansion and conquest throughout the Andes. The Incas, before the arrival of the Spaniards in South America, were one of the greatest cultures that developed in the economic, political, social, and religious aspects.

THE INCA TRAIL TO MACHU PICCHU

CHAPTER III
THE INCAS BEFORE THE ARRIVAL OF THE SPANISH

According to the studies carried out by historian Waldemar Espinoza Soriano in his work *"The Incas, Economy, Society, and State in the Age of Tahuantinsuyo"* (1997), the Incas, until before the arrival of the Spaniards, were divided into two: the mythical Incas and the historical Incas. The Incas, until before the arrival of the Spaniards, were divided into two: the mythical Incas and the historical Incas.

Mythical Incas

Why their origin is covered by a mythical and religious mantle: they are Manco Capac, Sinchi Roca, Lloque Yupanqui, Mayta Capac, Capac Yupanqui, Inca Roca, Yahuar Huacac, and Wiracocha.

Manco Capac

Manco Capac, will be the first mythical Inca, also known by the name of Ayar Manco. He was the one who managed to place the Taipicala ethnic group in the valley of Cusco, evicting the local ethnic groups such as the Huallas and Sahuaseras from their lands.

Manco Capac faced constant fights against the ethnic groups of the Ayarmacas, who saw the Incas as invaders of their lands. It was the same Manco Capac, who was confronted with Tocay Capac and Pinagua Capac leaders of the ethnic group of the Ayarmacas.

THE INCA TRAIL TO MACHU PICCHU

Manco Capac, the first Inca. Drawing by Felipe Guaman Poma de Ayala, "Nueva Coronica y Buen Gobierno", 1615.

This constant struggle between Incas and Ayarmacas was very tense and persistent. Manco Capac when not being able to conquer more neighboring ayllus spent the rest of his life until his death in the coexistence of his wives, Mama Ocllo and Mama Huaco, and their children. It was with Mama Ocllo, with whom he had his son Sinchi Roca, who would be named the new Inca.

Manco Capac, ordered to divide the area occupied in the valley of Cusco, into four neighborhoods; Quinticancha, Chumbicancha, Sairecancha, and Yarambuycancha, where the halves of each neighborhood were divided in two, taking each one, the name of Hanancuscos and Hurincuscos. Manco Capac kept the name "CAPAC", or king, as a sign of the power of his ancestors, the Taipicalas.

Upon the death of Manco Capac, his corpse was mummified and placed in the *Inticancha* until the government of the Inca Pachacuteq, who ordered the transfer of the mummy to the temple of Lake Titicaca.

Manco Capac, is very important for the information of the Spanish chronicles, which give us, as the founder of the dynasty of the Incas, along with this religious mysticism about the origin of the empire of the Incas, taking as the main god the Sun. To give his origin as a sacred son descended from the father *Inti*, or Sun God.

CHAPTER III: THE INCAS BEFORE THE ARRIVAL OF THE SPANIARDS

Sinchi Roca

Son of Manco Capac. At birth, he was given the name of Roca, but because of his conditions of strong man and warrior, or *sinchi*, upon the death of his father and then take power, he was given the name of Sinchi Roca.

Before arriving at the valley of Cusco, his father Manco Capac, had married him with the daughter of the lord of the ayllu of Saño, the current District of San Sebastian, Mama Coca. Sinchi Roca, like his father, advanced towards the valley of Cusco, but when he arrived he confronted the local people who saw them as invaders. Product of these warlike confrontations, he lost some teeth with some of the chiefs of the Ayarmacas that covered a great area of the valley of Cusco.

Sinchi Roca. Drawing by Felipe Guaman Poma de Ayala, "Nueva Coronica y Buen Gobierno", 1615.

Sinchi Roca could not be called Inca, because his territorial domain was very small. He only managed to conquer the territories near the Singa hill, in the current Inca complexes of Tambomachay and Puka Pukara.

When Sinchi Roca died, Manco Sapaca should have succeeded him, but for unknown reasons, he was replaced by Lloque Yupanqui, as the new leader of this human group.

Lloque Yupanqui

Sinchi Roca's son, like his father, continued with this process of expansion and conquest of new towns and territories, confronting his new enemies: the Ayarmacas. These were people with greater territorial expansion, who saw the new conquerors as invaders.

Lloque Yupanqui managed to ally with other small ethnic groups, gaining the confidence of the local chiefs through marriages with the wives or daughters of the local chiefs, all motivated by a desire for personal convenience. He managed to conquer the lands of the ayllus of Maras, as well as other neighboring territories.

Lloque Yupanqui. Drawing by Felipe Guaman Poma de Ayala, "Nueva Coronica y Buen Gobierno", 1615.

Lloque Yupanqui took as his wife the daughter of the curaca of the ayllu of Oma who called herself Mama Cagua. Creating in the groups of the ayllus of Ayarmacas a lot of distrust, fights, and confrontations, increasing their dominion of the Incas to other territories.

Upon the death of Lloque Yupanqui, he was succeeded by a fourth son named Mayta Capac, thus maintaining control of the Hurin hierarchy or religious power.

Mayta Capac

Mayta Capac, arrived at the power of his curacazgo, being very young. Due to his youth, he was replaced by one of his uncles. It was at this time when the Alcahuisa ethnic group, led by the Ayar

CHAPTER III: THE INCAS BEFORE THE ARRIVAL OF THE SPANIARDS

Ucho, rebelled to regain their freedom and evict the Incas from their lands.

When the Alcahuisas were defeated and Ayar Ucho was captured as a prisoner, he was locked up in a perpetual prison until his death. Defeated the Alcahuisas, the Incas strengthened their power in the Cusco valley, which remained a small curacazgo. This occupation by the Inca ethnic group annoyed the local ethnic groups because they were deprived of arable land, water distribution, and control of grazing areas for camelids.

Mayta Capac. Drawing by Felipe Guaman Poma de Ayala, "Nueva Coronica y Buen Gobierno", 1615.

Mayta Capac, increased his political, military, and religious power during his reign. He had as heir his son Tarco Huaman, a product of the alliance with the daughter of the daughter of the chief of the Collaguas, or Caillomas. Tarco Huaman was deposed by his cousin Capac Yupanqui. Like his father, he expanded the ethnic group, which was still small.

Capac Yupanqui

Cápac Yupanqui was the nephew of Mayta Cápac and cousin of Tarco Huaman. He was not the son of the main woman of Mayta Capac, but one of the concubines of the Inca ethnic group.

When the new sovereign came to power, he ordered to kill all the brothers of Tarco Huaman so that none of the heirs would claim the succession. And to the other chiefs of the ayllus, he ordered them to be loyal to his government.

During their reign, he began to organize expeditions to local towns with the eagerness to win bigger territories, planning battles, arriving to conquer the territories of the Cuntis, toward the Collasuyo, the territories of Quechuas of Abancay. Before the advance of the Chancas of Ayacucho, toward the valley of Cusco, he left in the area of Abancay to his cousin Tarco Huaman, who had the task of guarding this territory and sending 1,000 exotic birds for their religious ceremonies.

Capac Yupanqui knew how to take advantage of this situation of fame, the reason for which the curacazgo of the Ayarmacas, which at that time was a very large village, sent in marriage to his daughter Curi Hilpay, the alliance that was favorable for the Inca ethnic group.

Cusi Chimbo, Mayta Capac's wife, was the one who poisoned him out of personal jealousy. This act was planned by Roca, future Inca Roca, his brother, and a cousin or chief of ayllu belonging to the Hanan.

This social and political situation was taken advantage of by the Chancas, who invaded the Quechua area of Abancay. At the death of Capac Yupanqui, it is very important to mention that the domain of the Hurin, the religious social class, ended. Since then, the Hanan ethnic group took political, social, military, and religious control.

Inca Roca

To the death of Cápac Yupanqui, they are the ayllus of the Hanan that begin to take the power of the Inca ethnic group, taking the Inticancha, as their residence. It is this way to strengthen this domain of power on the part of the Hanan, they proclaimed with the name of "Inca" to one of their leaders, being Inca Roca,

CHAPTER III: THE INCAS BEFORE THE ARRIVAL OF THE SPANIARDS

the first Inca, a title that was given to the leader with greater power. The Inca married the wife of Capac Yupanqui, Cusi Chimbo.

Inca Roca, began with this process of recovery of political, social, military, and their ancestors, the Taipicalas. He left strictly the religious domain to the ayllus of the Hurin. The Inticancha followed its specific space and was later the place where the main priests lived.

Inca Roca. Drawing by Felipe Guaman Poma de Ayala, "Nueva Coronica y Buen Gobierno", 1615.

Inca Roca had his residence built elsewhere, establishing the tradition that each future Inca would build his palace or residence.

The recovery of power by the Hanan ayllus motivated them to continue with this process of territorial expansion, confronting their bitter adversaries, the ethnic groups of the Ayarmacas, in fierce battles.

The Chancas also continued in this process of territorial expansion to invade the valley of Cusco, territory occupied by the ethnic groups of the Ayarmacas and Incas. The problem of Inca Roca was not to leave in the conquered lands of garrisons or surveillance posts in the conquered places.

In Cusco, Inca Roca improved the water canalization system, ordering the construction of water canals for the water supply to the Cusco valley and the cultivation terraces. He instituted places of education for the young upper class to learn weapons, handling

Palace of Inca Roca, Hatun Rumiyoc Street, Cusco.

of the *quipus*, or accounting system, and learning the language, such as Puquina and Quechua.

The curacazgo of the Inca ethnic group continued being very small before the attentive look of the Ayarmacas, which occupied the Cusco valley and the area of Anta. To avoid future confrontations between both ethnic groups, the Ayarmacas, and the Incas, the chiefs of these ethnic groups, made exchanges of women like Mama Chiquia, daughter of Tocay Cápac, with Tito Cusi Yupanqui. Curi Ocllo, daughter of Inca Roca, was given to the king of the Ayarmacas, establishing an alliance in the interest of political and territorial dominance.

Yahuar Huacac

Inca Roca had several sons. One of them was Tito Cusi Huallpa. When he came to power, he took the name of Yahuar Huacac, or "cry of blood". Being a child, Titu Cusi Yupanqui was taken prisoner

CHAPTER III: THE INCAS BEFORE THE ARRIVAL OF THE SPANIARDS

by the Ayarmacas and when the chief of these commanded to kill this child, he cried with blood tears, before which he forgave him and sent him to raise camelids.

Yahuar Huacac, when arriving in the power of the Inca ethnic group, had a short period of his reign. He conquered some villages such as the Pinaguas, who revolted. However, they were submitted thanks to the tip of one of the brothers of Yahuar Huacac called Vicaquirao, who advised the Inca that to each conquered place they should build garrisons for territorial control. He also conquered other places occupied by the Cuntis.

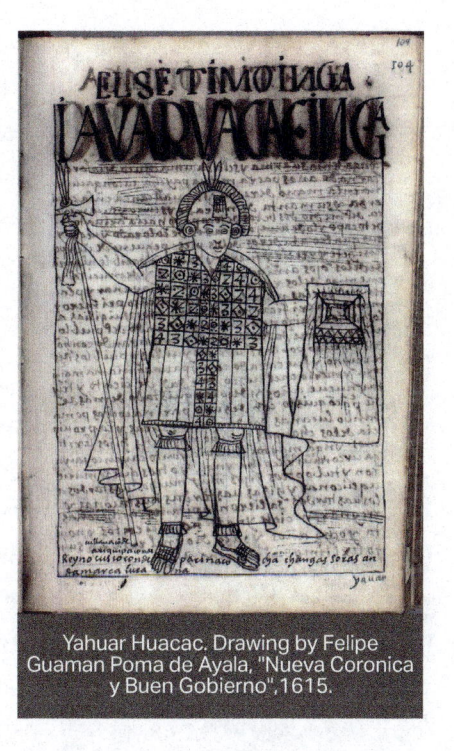

Yahuar Huacac. Drawing by Felipe Guaman Poma de Ayala, "Nueva Coronica y Buen Gobierno",1615.

Yahuar Huacac, with the children he had with Mama Chiquia, chose as future Inca his son Paguac Huallpa, who was murdered by the ethnic group of the Huallacanes. Upon learning of this fact, Yahuar Huacac ordered the destruction of the town of Paulo and commanded to kill those responsible.

He organized an expedition of conquest towards the zone of the Collasuyo, by the Titicaca lake. However, to the uprising of many ethnic groups of the Cuntis, this idea was destabilized. The Cuntis, taking advantage of the festivity carried out by the Incas, attacked the Cusco valley and took the Inticancha. In this place Yahuar Huacac was assassinated, along with several of his sons, thus creating a great political and religious confusion in the reign of the Incas.

These episodes give us a good idea that the Inca ethnic group was still small and threatened by the local ethnic groups as well as the great power of the Chancas of Apurimac.

Wiracocha

To the death of Yahuar Huacac on the part of the ethnic groups of the Cuntis, a great confusion was established in the Inca ethnic group on who should be the new sovereign. At the proposal of some local ethnic groups, they named Jatun Topac as Inca, who was not Yahuar Huacac's son. But to maintain the dominance of the Hanan class, he was presented as if he was to be named the new *Sapa Inca*.

Jatun Topac, took the *mascaypacha* as the new Inca, assuming the name of Wiracocha, to pretend that he was a descendant of the God of the same name: the main divinity of the Taipicala, giving it a mythical and religious character.

Wiracocha. Drawing by Felipe Guaman Poma de Ayala, "Nueva Coronica y Buen Gobierno", 1615.

Wiracocha took as his main wife Mama Runto, daughter of the chief of Anta, with whom he had as son Cusi Yupanqui, the future Pachacúteq, who would be the great conqueror of the Inca State.

In their eagerness for expansion of the Inca territory, he arrived to conquer the lands of Calca and Yucay, facing the residents of the area of Pisac (Pacha and Pocoy). Wiracocha counted on the military direction of Vicaquirao and Apo Maita, who were his uncles.

CHAPTER III: THE INCAS BEFORE THE ARRIVAL OF THE SPANIARDS

This is how the Inca ethnic group began to have greater political, military, and religious power. But at the same time the ayllus of the Hurin, tried to recover their political, military, and religious dominion creating mutinies, conspiracies with the Chancas that appeared in the Cusco valley. These rebellions had to be controlled during the period of his government.

The reign of Wiracocha is a time of great social tension. The Inca ordered to build in the upper part of the Vilcanota valley, nowadays between the villages of Lamay and Calca, his palace. As the tradition was that each Inca had to build his palace, he increased the cultivated land. This is the Vilcanota Valley or Sacred Valley of the Incas, introducing the new rules to the conquered peoples.

When conquering the south of Cusco, in the provinces of Canchis, he ordered to build a great temple dedicated to the god *Tecsi Wiracocha*, near the city of Sicuani, in the area of San Pedro. He advanced toward the territories of the Collasuyo, leaving in his replacement in the valley of Cusco to one of his sons named Urco, who lacked all the ambition of expansion and conquest of his predecessors, allowing himself to fall into the vice of drunkenness and women.

The Cusco valley continued to be threatened by the invasion of the Chancas, reaching its borders as far as the Apurimac River, which to a certain extent kept the two ethnic groups apart. However, the Chancas had greater political, military, and territorial dominance.

At this point, we want to refer to the government of the "Inca Urco", who was appointed by his father Wiracocha as his successor, being named as the new Inca, taking the maskaypacha as a symbol of power. At the same time, the Chancas were advancing towards the Cusco valley area, to annex them to their territorial domain.

When he was appointed as the new ruler, the Inca Urco began to rule the Inca ethnic group, while his father Wiracocha, went to spend his old age, far away, in his room located in the area of Huchuy Qosqo, or the city of *small Cusco*, in the heights of Lamay and Calca.

The Inca Urco did not continue with the process of territorial expansion. Rather, he dedicated himself to frivolous pleasures, such as drinking until he was drunk, vomiting and urinating in the streets, like any other adolescent, without character and personality, having sexual relations with any woman who came his way, and without respect for social classes. He got involved with the *mamaconas*, who, at that time, were women very respected by the Inca State, generating the discontent of many chiefs of the Inca ethnic group, who wanted to dethrone him. But fearing to be annihilated by their father Wiracocha, these chiefs abandoned this idea.

At this political and social juncture, the Chancas saw a great opportunity to invade the valley of Cusco, reaching Vilcacunca. The situation of many ethnic groups that were close to the Apu-

Archaeological complex of Huchuy Qosqo, a small city near Cusco, located in the heights of the Sacred Valley of the Incas, between Calca and Lamay, Cusco.

rimac River was one of anxiety and fear since they did not have the support of the Cusco ethnic group. These were originally from the Castrovirreina area, in the current region of Huancavelica, descendants of the Paqarina of Lake Choclococha (4,950 meters/16,682 feet). Like the Incas, they came from the highlands to settle in the fertile valleys to dominate fertile lands and control various ecological levels. Their leader Uscovilca, who was the founder of the kingdom of the Chancas, had the vision of expanding his territories from Huancavelica to the southeast, advancing to the lands of Andahuaylas probably at the beginning of the 13th century.

The Chancas, at the beginning of the 15th century, was the dominant of the territories of Huancavelica, Ayacucho, Apurímac, and some territories of Arequipa. Thus, they were ready to invade the lands of the Ayarmacas and Incas ethnic groups, whose territorial space was between the valleys of Cusco, Vilcanota, and the Pampas of Anta. Ayarmacas and Incas were in a state of great political, social and religious tension, since the ayllus of the Hurin, wanted to recover the political dominion of the Inca ethnic group that was under the control of the ayllus of the Hanan.

This is where one of the third sons of the Inca Wiracocha arises. His name: Titu Cusic Yupanqui. When he saw the situation of danger, he called the other ethnic groups of the valley of Cusco and the ethnic groups of the pampa of Anta, where his mother Mama Runto was from, so that they united to fight against this invasion of the Chancas.

Thanks to the myth that the rocks became soldiers, he defeated the Chancas in a great battle in the lands of Ichupampa, which would later be called Yahuarpampa, or "plain of blood".

To the great triumph of the Inca ethnic group, with the support of the ethnic groups of Anta and others, the Incas were able to defeat and destroy the Chanca people, thus removing Inca Urco.

The Inca Wiracocha was not entirely happy that Titu Cusic Yupanqui was named the new Inca, but due to pressure from the local ethnic groups, he had to accept Titu Cusic Yupanqui as the new master, who upon taking the maskaypacha, took the name of Pachacúteq, meaning the *Transformer* and *Rebuilder of the Earth.*

It is from Pachacúteq that the ethnic group of the Incas, which, until then, covered the valleys of Cusco and Vilcanota, thanks to the expansion and conquest, ceased to be an ethnic group or small lordship to become a great State called the *Tawantinsuyo*, or "the empire of the four regions" of the world.

The historical Incas

Because their origin is written in history, for their exploits, conquests, expansion, and construction of large urban and religious cities, which gave rise to the creation of the great empire of the Incas: they are Titu Cusic Yupanqui (the future Pachacuteq), Inca Amaru Yupanqui, Túpac Yupanqui, Huayna Cápac, Huáscar, and Atahuallpa.

Cusi Yupanqui (Pachacuteq) (1438 - 1471)

It is from Pachacuteq that we start talking about the historical Incas, since history mentions him in all its sources (chronicles of the XVI and XVII centuries), especially the Inca Pachacúteq, as "Transformer of the Uni-

Cusi Yupanqui, or Pachacúteq. Drawing by Felipe Guaman Poma de Ayala, "Nueva Coronica y Buen Gobierno", 1615.

verse", comparing him with Alexander the Great, another great conqueror of the Old World, who conquered Europe, Asia, and Africa.

As we have said, his birth name was Cusi Yupanqui, third son of the Inca Wiracocha and Mama Runto, daughter of the lord of Anta. Mama Runto was the main wife of the Inca Wiracocha, but he had more children with his concubines or secondary women, who had more influence in the political decisions of the Inca.

When Wiracocha retired to his quarters in Calca, he appointed Urco as the new ruler of the Inca ethnic group. He took the *maskaypacha* as a symbol of political and religious power. Inca Urco did not follow the tradition of his ancestors of conquering new territories to consolidate the Inca dominion. On the contrary, he dedicated himself to mundane tasks of every human being, sex, and alcohol, causing the discontent of many chiefs of ayllus and ethnic groups of the valley of Cusco, for which they tried to dethrone him.

However, the threat of invasion by the Chancas towards the valley of Cusco, motivated one of the sons of Wiracocha, called Cusi Yupanqui, to take up arms, calling for a confederation of the ayllus and ethnic groups to confront the Chancas. Thus, in the Pampa de Anta (Ichupampa), the rocks became brave soldiers to confront and destroy the Chancas in the battle of Yahuarpampa.

It is important to mention that according to mythical history, the Sun God told Cusi Yupanqui in a dream that he would come to his aid to defeat the Chancas. This dream was explained to the ethnic groups that with the power of the Sun God, they would defeat the Chancas. Incas and Ayarmacas united to defeat the invaders. The ethnic groups of Anta, where his mother was from, helped Cusi Yupanqui to defeat the fierce Chancas.

Pachacuteq, having all the support of the local ethnic groups of the Cusco valley, the Vilcanota valley and the Anta pampas, and the divine power of the Sun God, began the stage of transformation, reorganization of a simple local curacazgo to what would be until before the arrival of the Spanish invaders as a great State soon called the Tawantinsuyo.

In Inticancha, he married Mama Anahuarque, taking her as his main wife. But, during his long reign, he also had countless secondary wives. It is said that at the death of the Inca Pachacuteq he had in all the Inca territory more than 200 or 300 children, showing that in each place that he conquered he immediately took a woman as a concubine as part of his harem to establish the alliance with the conquered peoples.

Monument to the Inca Pachacuteq, main square of Machu Picchu Pueblo.

CHAPTER III: THE INCAS BEFORE THE ARRIVAL OF THE SPANIARDS

To begin with this process of conquest, he had his half-brother Inca Urco eliminated from the official history of the Incas as one of the great errors committed that discredited the Incas belonging to the Hanan ethnic groups.

Once the Chancas were defeated, Pachacúteq began the task of conquering the towns of the Cusco valley and other neighboring territories to consolidate his power. He advanced towards the complete conquest of the Vilcanota valley, reaching the territories of Ollantaytambo, Piccho, a place that is mentioned in the Spanish chronicles where the Inca citadel of Machu Picchu would be located, Vitcos, Vilcabamba, and Amaybamba (Antisuyo), places that had fertile valleys for the cultivation of corn, potatoes, and the sacred coca leaf, as well as other agricultural products.

Pachacuteq organized his first expedition of conquest towards the territories of the Chinchaysuyo that were the territories occupied by the defeated Chancas in the valley of Andahuaylas and other towns like Cotanera, Cotapampa, Aymaraes, and Omasayo, all located in the current department of Apurímac. Then, he advanced towards the coastal area, where he conquered and annexed the Chinchas, Nazcas, and Lunaguanas, where he ordered to build a city, or *llaqta*, with the name of Incahuasi.

The Inca Pachacuteq had begun his conquest stage with great success. Many ethnic groups joined this process of growth. After the Chinchaysuyo, he advanced towards the south of Cusco, to the territories of the Collasuyo, to impede the advance of the reigns of the Collao and Lupacas, leaving in these lands garrisons or control places to be informed about these kingdoms. On the side of the Contisuyo it arrived until Camana, the present city of Arequipa.

Pachacuteq expanded the territorial scope of the Incas. He even turned it into a great modern state. In each conquered place, he ordered the construction or reconstruction of cities, ceremonial sites such as Pachacamac, near the city of Lima, temples, bridges, roads, checkpoints, cultivation terraces, and other types of constructions.

In his thirty years of government, when he was already over 60 years old, he did a great job of construction and expansion, so it is necessary to mention:

He rebuilt Cusco, as the city of the Puma, turning it into a great imperial capital.

He transformed a small lordship located in the Cusco valley into what was a great state or empire, conquering large territories and fertile valleys. He expanded the influence of the Cusco valley, conquering the highlands and important valleys such as the Vilcanota and Andahuaylas, the coast as Nazca, and a part of the current city of Lima (Pachacamac). Then, they headed west towards the Collao, later called Collasuyo.

He rebuilt some population centers and ceremonial sites such as Pisac and Ollantaytambo.

The religious system changed. Before, there was a great variety of gods and goddesses. Thus, Pachacuteq named the Sun God, Inti, as the supreme god. Therefore, the Inca was considered the son of the Sun, giving him a mythical and religious character.

Until before Pachacuteq, in the Cusco valley and nearby territories, many languages were spoken, such as Quechua, Puquina, Aymara, and other local languages. Established in their government, the Quechua language became the official language throughout the *Incanato*. However, within the Inca upper class, it is possible that the important royal families spoke only the Puquina language.

He ordered to build in each conquered place, cities, like Machu Picchu, ceremonial places, like Sacsayhuaman, Tambomachay, Ollantaytambo and others, bridges, places of surveillance,

CHAPTER III: THE INCAS BEFORE THE ARRIVAL OF THE SPANIARDS

like Puka Pukara, Runkuraqay, cultivation platforms to Pisac, Ollantaytambo, Intipata, Moray, resting places, or *tampus*, as Qhanabamba,Qonchamarka, places of deposit, or *qollqas*, as Machu Qollqa, Ollantaytambo, and Inca roads, such as the road leading to the sacred city of Machu Picchu.

He rebuilt the Inticancha and changed the name to *Q'oricancha*, today, the current temple of Santo Domingo. The Q'oricancha became the most important ceremonial center in the entire Inca State. From Q'oricancha, all the Inca roads to the four regions into which the Tawantinsuyo was divided: the Antisuyo, the Collasuyo, the Contisuyo, and the Chinchaysuyo.

For political, religious, economic, and military control, he established a system of local chiefs in each conquered town throughout the state. These were to report to the central government of Cusco. He built ceremonial places, taking the Sun God as the main god while respecting the local gods in the conquered villages. He ordered the construction of cultivation terraces, thus dominating several ecological levels, taking as main products corn, potato, and coca leaf in the Antisuyo area, where the city of Machu Picchu is located.

In the military aspect, all the conquered peoples had to send as a sign of tribute not only flora and fauna resources but also young people, who would be trained and prepared to form the powerful Inca army.

To connect all the conquered Inca territory until the government of Pachacuteq, he ordered the construction of a whole system of roads, which varied according to their geographical location of punas, mountains, valleys, jungle, and coast. They varied in distances and spaces, long, wide, short, or very narrow, many of them paved and others with marks or signs especially in the coastal area. This is because the territory of the Andes is not flat. The Andes mountain range covers a great variety of altitudinal floors from the glaciers, at more than 6,000 meters above sea level (more than 20,220 feet) up to the coastal area, dominating several ecological floors in terms of flora, fauna, climate, land quality and raw material for the construction of these roads.

The Incan Empire covered a large territorial area until before the arrival of the Spaniards. Today, the current countries, to the north, with Colombia and Ecuador, to the south, with Chile and Argentina, to the east, with Bolivia, and to the west with current Peru.

Being old, Pachacúteq left as co-ruler to his son Túpac Yupanqui, who had been conquering other places, who would later follow in his father's footsteps, continuing with all the Inca legacy implied.

The "Transformer of the Universe", continued with his task of construction, innovation, transformation in all aspects from the political to the social. At his death, he had left a great legacy throughout the Andes, establishing a great state, which many researchers call the Inca Empire or culture, but for local archaeologists, they call it the Tahuantinsuyo Empire or culture.

The son of the Sun is thus the "reconstructor" of the extraordinary Inca state that developed in the Peruvian Andes.

Inka Amaru Yupanqui

Son of Pachacuteq with the Coya Anawarqe, who, during the government of his father, accompanied him in different campaigns and military expeditions. He conquered villages in the Altiplano area (Lake Titicaca) as Karakara, Paria, Pokona, Charka, Chicha, Chuy, villages that are currently in Bolivia, strengthening the Inca power in that territory.

Inka Amaru Yupanqui was commissioned by his father to conquer the territories of the Guarani, peoples who lived in the

CHAPTER III: THE INCAS BEFORE THE ARRIVAL OF THE SPANIARDS

territories of Brazil, Bolivia, and Argentina, at that time. When this expedition failed, he was replaced by one of his brothers called Túpac Yupanqui, who was also supported by other royal families or the main *panacas* of the Cusco region.

Tupac Inca Yupanqui (1471 - 1493)

Tupac Inca Yupanqui took command at the adult age of more than 30 years. At the death of the Inca Pachacúteq, he was appointed as the new Sapa of the Inca State, for which he organized a serie of celebrations including sacrifices of children and llamas.

Tupac Inca Yupanqui, like his father, carried out a great political and military task, conquering other territories, expanding other regions especially towards the Antisuyo area, towards the jungle, integrating settlements that could provide exotic birds feathers, medicinal plants, coca leaf, which was a highly appreciated product by the Inca settlers, and *chonta* wood for the manufacture of weapons of war.

Tupac Yupanqui. Drawing by Felipe Guaman Poma de Ayala, "Nueva Coronica y Buen Gobierno",1615.

During his reign, occured uprisings or revolts of the people of the territory of Lake Titicacaca, for which he had to leave the city of Cusco to consolidate that part of the territory, calming the rebellion of many local villages such as the Callahuayas, Capachicas, and Omasuyos. He managed to consolidate his political and military power up to the area of Chacarmarca, the current Desaguadero, reaching Chile and the north of Argentina.

The Inca Tupac Yupanqui was at the origin of the division of the empire into four dictated regions. The union of these four regions formed the Tahuantinsuyo, being the city of Cusco, as political capital.

As the legacy or tradition of the Inca rulers was to have several concubines or secondary wives. He was poisoned by one of them, named Chuqui Ocllo, who did not accept that the prince Tito Cusi Huallpa (Huayna Capac), be appointed as the new ruler. At his death, Tupac Inca Yupanqui was mummified and taken to the town of Chinchero, a town existing today at 1 hour and 20 minutes from the city of Cusco.

The town of Chinchero is very famous because its inhabitants continue to maintain the tradition and customs of the Inca era and once a week, on Sunday, you can observe the local trade, the famous barter (exchange of products), where it is not necessary to use money.

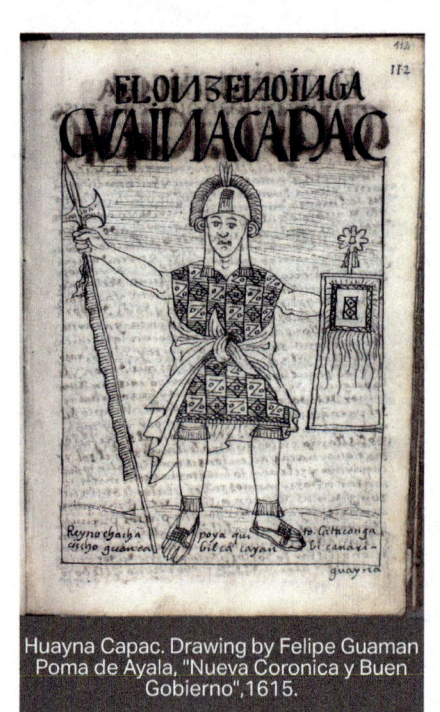

Huayna Capac. Drawing by Felipe Guaman Poma de Ayala, "Nueva Coronica y Buen Gobierno",1615.

Huayna Capac (1493 - 1527)

Tito Cusi Huallpa came to power after the death of his father. He received the support of his mother, Mama Ocllo, who had the support of one of the Inca generals of

CHAPTER III: THE INCAS BEFORE THE ARRIVAL OF THE SPANIARDS

The bases of the palace of Inca Huayna Capac are located behind the Palace of Justice in Cusco.

great respect, called Huaman Achache. The new Inca was persecuted and ordered to kill all the people who were involved in several insurrections at the time of the death of Tupac Inca Yupanqui. Calmed this uprising Tito Cusi Huallpa, took the name of Huayna Capac.

Upon assuming the government, the new Inca, like his ancestors, continued with the task of conquest and expansion. But, this time, he went to the north, that is to say, to the territories of the Chinchaysuyo, forming a multiregional army, with soldiers from different regions, conquering the local ethnic groups of Cayambes, Carangues, and Pastos, who after being conquered were transferred to the jungle area to dedicate themselves to the cultivation of the coca leaf.

He sent a large army to control the advance of the Guarani people coming from the south (Brazil, Bolivia, Argentina, and Chile), who wanted to conquer the Altiplano area (Lake Titicaca), building garrisons to protect the advance of these Amazonian peoples.

During the rule of the Inca Huayna Capac, the empire reached its maximum territorial expansion, conquering the territories of the current countries of Ecuador and southwestern Colombia. He remained for a long period in the northern territory where he built a llaqta, or city, called Inkapirka, which exists today in the city of Quito as an Inca complex.

Huayna Capac had the idea of wanting to divide Tawantinsuyo into two states for better control. But this idea did not materialize, keeping the city of Cusco as the only political capital of the empire. However, at the same time, there was great discontent from the royal families of the north who did not want Cusco to continue controlling the political and religious command.

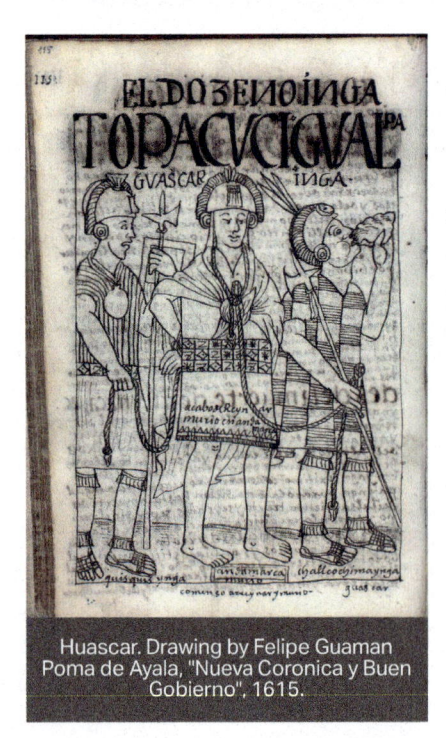

Huascar and Atahuallpa (1527 - 1533)

Huayna Capac had a son who was born south of the city of Cusco. His name was Topa Cusi Huallpa, he took the new name of Huascar and became the eleventh Inca.

When he became the new Inca, Huascar already had a great knowledge of political and administrative government, having at that time even the support of prince Atahuallpa who ruled

Huascar. Drawing by Felipe Guaman Poma de Ayala, "Nueva Coronica y Buen Gobierno", 1615.

CHAPTER III: THE INCAS BEFORE THE ARRIVAL OF THE SPANIARDS

in the northern part of the Chinchaysuyo region, present-day Ecuador.

During the rule of the Inca Huascar, the Incan Empire was framed in a territory of peace and tranquility co-governed in the northern regions by the prince Atahuallpa. It was a time when there were no more spaces to be conquered. The definitive borders of the Inca empire had been marked.

It is in this period that many families and villages did not agree with the Inca government. With the support of the northern nations, the prince Atahuallpa rises in rebellion against the power of his brother. He had the desire for power, who incited to rebel to the towns of the north like the Cayambes, the Carangues, and the Pastos. These towns had been subdued by the Incas at the time of Huayna Capac and they saw in Atahuallpa a way to recover their autonomy and territorial space.

Once this civil war began between Huascar and Atahuallpa, the Inca empire faced its great fall, a product of this war between the people of the north and the people of the south. To this was added the arrival of the Spanish invaders, who took advantage of this conflict between the two brothers. It would be easier to understand this way "divide and conquer". That is what the Spaniards did when they arrived in Tawantinsuyo.

Atahuallpa ordered his brother to be taken, prisoner. Huascar, being captive, all his

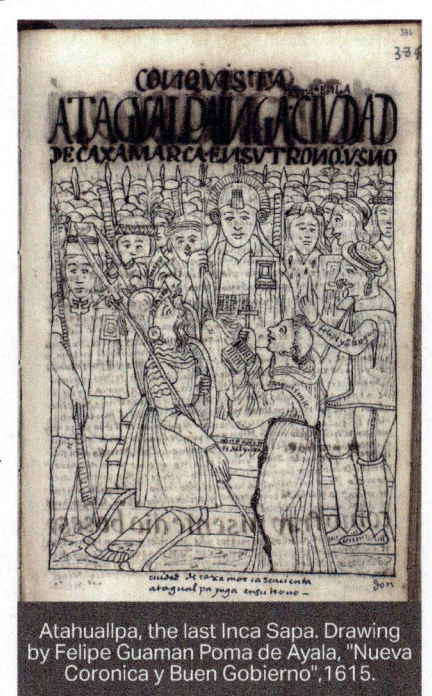

Atahuallpa, the last Inca Sapa. Drawing by Felipe Guaman Poma de Ayala, "Nueva Coronica y Buen Gobierno",1615.

81

family and children were ordered to be killed by the order of Atahuallpa, who wanted to erase the lineage of the legitimate Inca.

In 1532 the Spaniards arrived in Peru after organizing several expeditions to discover the great Inca State. When arriving at the city of Cajamarca they take the prisoner to Atahuallpa, who in prison ordered to execute Huascar, the fact that was not forgiven by the Spaniards, who knew to take advantage of all the existing conjuncture for than to ask for the "famous rescue of Atahuallpa": two rooms of silver and a room of gold.

It was ordered to take from all over the Inca empire especially from the ceremonial places, gold, and silver for the liberation of the then-new Inca Sapa, which was a big lie, since once these rooms were filled, Atahuallpa was destined to be assassinated for the death of his brother Huáscar, as well as other crimes.

This civil war between the brothers Huascar and Atahuallpa was the beginning of the fall of this great empire that was one of the most important and powerful cultures in this part of the world called South America. A culture that, at present, is still alive in its people and customs.

CHAPTER IV
THE RELIGION OF THE INCAS

To talk about the religion practiced by the Incas until the conquest of the Spaniards, we must place them in time and space. What religion did they practice and what gods did they have until the government of the Inca Pachacuteq? The ninth Inca established the god Inti, the Sun, as the absolute god throughout the empire. Of this, there remain material vestiges the constructions made in Machu Picchu, Cusco, or Pisac. However, other gods, such as the moon, the stars, the thunderbolt, the lightning, and the rainbow also belonged to the Inca pantheon at the end of the Empire.

A visible and palpable example is the Q'oricancha, the current Temple of Santo Domingo: worship to the huacas, or sacred rocks, to the mummies, or *mallquis*, to the *apus*, or sacred mountains, to the lakes, lagoons, rivers, springs, caves, local flora, and fauna. For them, the Incas built temples, sometimes with very fine and detailed architecture and others with simple architecture, with stones joined with mud mortar.

If we want to follow the evolutionary sequence of the development process of the Inca culture, empire, or State, we will have to start from its origin, with the creation of a simple local ethnic group that developed in the Cusco valley, until we reach the Tawantinsuyo.

The Q'oricancha, or temple of Santo Domingo, was built over the major temple of the Incas.

Religion in the valley of Cusco before the Inca Pachacúteq

According to the local archaeology of Cusco and archaeological findings located in different parts of Cusco and its provinces, it is known that before Pachacuteq, in the Cusco valley, there were groups of men who lived in caves or caverns, whose economy was based on hunting, grazing and raising camelids such as llamas, alpacas, guanacos, and vicuñas. Archaeology calls it the pre-ceramic period. The question would be: What kind of gods or religion did these men have? Their gods would be the stars, the moon, the sun, the lightning. Archaeology does not provide this type of information, which remains a mystery.

In the Formative period, when people came down from the highlands to the valleys, they began to settle in a territorial space. They began to cultivate and build their dwellings. They must have also built their ceremonial sites as a sign of gratitude. The men of the Formative, begin to manufacture their ceramics, with simple technology, in terms of the binder, type of firing, decorating them with geometric shapes, zoomorphic (felines) and anthropomorphic, and the use of colors. They built ceremonial places. We also have the same questions: what kind of gods or religion did the men of this time, such as the Marcavalles and Chanapatas, have?

In the period of the regional states, in the Cusco Valley, we have the Qotakallis, Killkis, and Lucres. These states will follow an evolutionary sequence having as ancestors the Marcavalles and Chanapatas. The Qotakallis, Killkis, and Lucres will begin to conquer other places outside the Cusco valley, reaching the Vilcanota valley. What Ollantaytambo and its surroundings are today, obviously looking for better places for the cultivation of corn, potatoes, and coca leaves. At the same time, they began to build roads to link these valleys. In their architecture, there is evidence of housing constructions and ceremonial centers like those of Ollantaytambo. The only evidence to understand the type of religious practice is through their ceramics. They are representing geometric and zoomorphic forms in their decoration. The question is also the same, what religion was practiced?

In the middle of the 8th century, the Waris invaded the Cusco valley. Proof of this is the archaeological site of Pikillaqta. It is a citadel with an architectural pattern and a very specific construction plan. The main enclosures were covered with plaster, showing a range of importance. The Waris, arriving from Ayacucho, will bring their religion, having as main gods Wiracocha and the Sun God, as they are a fusion of the Huarpa (Ayacucho), Nazca, and Tiananaco cultures. When they were expelled from the Cusco valley by the alliance of the Killkis and the Lucres, perhaps these regional states took the gods of the Waris since they influenced the ceramics, architecture, and construction throughout the valley.

If we follow the legends about the foundation of the Inca empire, the legend of Manco Capac and Mama Ocllo, or that of the Ayar brothers, we have the information of the chronicles of the 16th and 17th centuries. The Taipicalas, natives of Lake Titicaca, when evicted from their lands, begin this exodus northward towards the valley of Cusco, having as their main god Wiracocha (spiritual god, not visible, creator of the Universe), as the visible god, the Sun.

When they arrived at the lands of Pakareqtampu, they built their ceremonial places, surely preserving and practicing their religion of worship to Wiracocha and the Sun God. Then, when they arrived at the Cusco valley, in their process of conquest and having better cultivation fields, they met with the local ethnic groups, which must have had their religion such as the Ayarmacas, Pinaguas, Sahuaseras, and others. According to legends, the first chief of the Inca ethnic group to conquer the Cusco valley was Manco Capac, or Ayar Manco, who ordered the construction of the main temple, called the Inticancha, as a very important ceremonial center. This ethnic group was led by the Hurin (religious) Inca class, establishing the god Inti, the Sun, as their main god.

Several Inca belonging to the ethnic group of the Hurin, as Sinchi Roca, Lloque Yupanqui, and Mayta Cápac followed the Inca Manco Cápac. But it is in the government of the Inca Capac Yupanqui that a "coup d'etat" takes place, that of the Inca ethnic group of the Hanan. They take the power as their ancestors of the Taipicala, controlling everything at the political, military, and religious levels, following the rulers Inca Roca, Yahuar Huacac, Wiracocha, and Pachacuteq.

Pachacuteq, after defeating the Chancas, took the god Wiracocha as the main god and the Sun god as the visible god.

CHAPTER IV: THE RELIGION OF THE INCAS

According to historical sources, the god Wiracocha would be worshipped by the upper or privileged class, and the Sun god would be a state religion that would be practiced by all the people. An example of this would be the construction of the temple of Q'oricancha, from *Q'ori*, gold, and *cancha*, enclosure, which was built over the Inticancha, a temple built by the Hurin ethnic group.

It is from Pachacúteq that the Tawantinsuyo would have several gods and goddesses while worshipping other gods, establishing a polytheistic religion.

The religion of the Incas after the Inca Pachacuteq

By taking the maskaypacha, the Inca Pachacuteq, as a symbol of power, will restructure the religious apparatus, having as gods, Wiracocha, Inti, Killa (the Moon), Chaska (the Star), Illapa (the Lightning), and Kuychi (the Rainbow), as well as other gods or goddesses, such as Pachamama (Mother Nature), Pachacamac (the God of Fire), or Mama Cocha (the Goddess of Water). They will also worship the apus (the sacred mountains), the mallquis (the mummies), the huacas (the sacred rocks), and other local gods practiced by the conquered peoples.

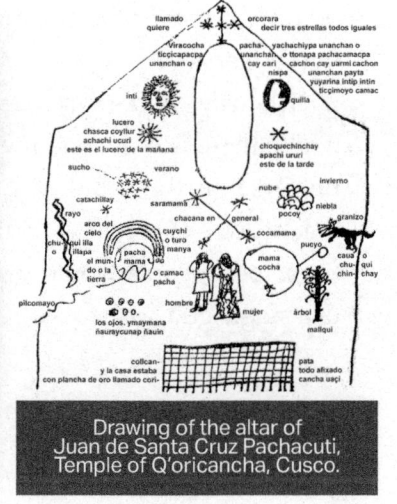

Imitation of the altar of Juan de Santa Cruz Pachacuti. Temple of Q'oricancha, Cusco.

Drawing of the altar of Juan de Santa Cruz Pachacuti, Temple of Q'oricancha, Cusco.

Wiracocha, the Creator of the Universe

Wiracocha, Creator God, was brought by the Hurin and Hanan ethnic groups from the Taipicala territory (Lake Titicaca) to the Cusco valley.

This deity, possibly in the time of the Incas, was a god worshiped only by the upper class, having the Sun god as a state god. This referred to the common class, which they did not take as the only god, since they continued to worship their local gods.

The real name of Wiracocha, according to the Spanish chronicles, would be "Illa Tecsi Apu Kontiki Wiracocha Pacha Yachachin". Each word has its meaning, which we will separate for a better understanding:

Illa, the light, the radiance, Tecsi, the origin or divine principle, Apu Kontiki, the Lord, protector or guardian. And Wiracocha, in the same way, to understand it would have to be divided into two words: *Wira*, which means bait, oil, and *Cocha* which means water, water foam. Thus, Wiracocha would mean "foam on the water", or "being that walks on top of the water". Pacha Yachasin would be "the computer and creator of the universe".

Then "Illa Tecsi Apu Kontiki Wiracocha Pacha Yachachin" would be translated as "the eternal Light, the Principle, divine origin spirit over the waters, Lord God Creator and Ordainer of the Universe".

In a way, Wiracocha was very similar to the Catholic religion, where there is only one invisible God, who is the creator of the universe, in the same way. That was the main reason why, in that process of conquest by the Spaniards towards the Inca settlers, these local people would very easily accept the Christian concept of a single god.

Inti, the Sun

Upon taking power and command of the Incas, it is the Inca Pachacuteq who takes the Sun god as a god of conquest and dominion over the defeated peoples. The Inti appears as a visible god, or material, which can be seen but cannot be touched, thus being the Sun as the god of the popular classes. On the foundations of the Inticancha (from *inti*; sun and *cancha*; enclosure), the Sapa Inca would build a new temple called the Q'oricancha (the current Dominican temple of Santo Domingo). It was in the Q'oricancha where several temples were built, one of which was the main temple dedicated to the Sun God, the official deity symbolizing the Tawantinsuyo.

The Sun was considered as a fertilizer god of the earth. Thus Pachacúteq and his successors were seen as the "Sons of the Sun God", giving them a divine and religious character, which was the call to make all this change and transformation of the Inca people. Which was represented in the Q'oricancha in the form of a golden disc: the *Punchao*. The Spanish conquistadors took possession of it when they invaded Cusco in 1533. We lose track of this sacred object after the capture of the young Tupac Amaru, in 1572, during the relentless repression of the rebellion of the successors of Atahuallpa.

In every conquered town or every important place, a temple to the Sun was built. Some of them have survived the ravages of time. Thus, some Inca sites have preserved, even today, temples dedicated to the god Inti. This is the case of Pisac or Machu Picchu.

Killa, the Moon

Considered in the religion of the Incas as the wife and sister of the Sun God, she was linked to the sea or waters. In the coastal zone, for pre-Inca cultures such as the Mochicas and Chimus, the

Moon Goddess was the one who governed the behavior of the sea or the water element, perhaps because one of their main economies was fishing. The Moon and the Sun would be the creatures of Tecsi Wiracocha. And it is in the Q'oricancha where a temple was built in her honor, which was represented by a disk made of silver. It is also represented by the plate mentioned by the chronicler Pachacuti Santa Cruz, on the left side of the God Wiracocha. In the time of the Incas, ceremonies such as the feast of Coya Raymi, with feasts and offerings.

Temple of the Sun, Q'oricancha, Cusco.

Chaska, the Star

In the Q'oricancha, there is a temple dedicated to this deity Chaska, the Star.

At the time of the colony, this temple of the stars was hidden by the Dominican priests, with the idea of erasing the Inca religion from the local inhabitants. This temple has in its middle part, facing the main square, a trapezoidal access opening, which is well carved, presenting on both sides, several holes. According to Dr. Luis Barreda Murillo, these would have been carved to place offerings such as seashells or precious stones. This access opening is oriented towards the Winter Solstice, on June 21, which would be one of the main festivities in the time of the Incas.

CHAPTER IV: THE RELIGION OF THE INCAS

Illapa, the Lightning

He is the god of the rains. Illapa would be linked to lightning, thunder, and lightning bolt as one. According to Luis Barreda Murillo, the populations of the Collasuyo, relate him to the famous Choque

Temple of Relampago, Q'oricancha, Cusco.

Chinchay, as the good god, who brings water from the sky. But he is also related to the hailstones, as the bad god, because he destroys the corn and potato crops. So before having the rains, it comes from the sky with thunder, lightning, and thunderbolt, causing fear among humans. The Incas captured this representation of the god Illapa in the ceremonial center of Sacsayhuaman, with its zigzagging forms in its first level of construction.

Kuychi, the Rainbow

The Rainbow, within the Inca religion, would be the bridge that unites the infrahuman world with the celestial world. A means by which one can ascend and descend, an effective instrument for the healer to catch the souls of sick people.

The rainbow is associated with the element of water and the Milky Way as the umbilical cord of cosmic union. The Spanish chronicles refer to the rainbow as an axis of supernatural power and especially of a protective divinity of the Inca.

In the Q'oricancha, where there is a building dedicated to this deity, according to the Spanish chronicles this enclosure had inside walls painted in bright colors. To its ceiling, hung a large number of crystals that with the movement of the wind produced a colorful rainbow inside.

Pachacamac, the god of Movement

Pachacamac was considered as the god that gives movement to the earth, controller of seismic movements. He was a god that was venerated in the coastal area. Pachacamac was a very important ceremonial place along the coast until the arrival of the Incas who came from the Cusco valley.

In the process of expansion of the Inca Pachacuteq towards the territories of the Contisuyo, to conquer the Chinchas and move northward towards the Chinchaysuyo, there was already in these lands, a very important religious place called Pachacamac.

The much larger temple was built over this ceremonial center, which continued to maintain its importance. This temple would be dedicated to the god Wiracocha, the god of the Inca ethnic group. This temple was built with adobe bricks. And to the conquest of the Spaniards, in their eagerness to replace the religion of the Incas by the Catholic religion, they are going to replace by the Lord of Miracles, denominating him, as the Lord of Pachacamilla. This is easy to understand since the conqueror imposes his new religion and culture on the defeated people.

Pachamama, Mother Earth

Pachamama, Mother Earth, or Mother Nature, considered as the goddess of fertility, was the one who provided food to her children who were human beings as well as to the animals. On her surface human beings build their houses, temples, terraces, and roads. It is the place where the dead are buried underground, where the cycle of life began.

CHAPTER IV: THE RELIGION OF THE INCAS

Pachamama was venerated by the pre-Inca peoples, in Inca times, colonial times, and up to the present day. Every year, in August, she is venerated using an offering that the local inhabitants nowadays call "payment to the Earth", this so that the farmer has enough corn, potato, and coca production the following year, during the harvest season; and that the shepherds have more llamas and alpacas. The current man continues with his tradition, making his offerings (payments or dispatches), to have more work, good health, love, money, and others.

The Inca calendar was agricultural. For the Incas, and the local people today, the month of August was and remains the first month of their year, as we are close to the planting season and the rainy season, which makes more sense today. It is in honor to the Pachamama that the most important offerings were the *mullus*, or seashells, which symbolize the water element, the sacred coca leaf, the *wira*, or llama or alpaca bait, corn seeds, cotton, flowers, and the aja, or chicha, which was offered at the beginning and the end of the ceremony, inviting the apus and the Tayta Inti, the Sun God.

Apachetas

The apachetas, are pylons made with stones of different sizes that are placed one on top of the other, symbolizing dreams and desires that one wants in life. These apachetas were placed on the roads, ceremonial places, or in the "passes", the highest points between two valleys.

Even today, we can still see them on the Inca trail to Machu Picchu (first and second pass) and many other places. The word "apacheta", is a more Castilianized word, being in the Inca language, Quechua, "apay" which would mean, bring, take, carry, and "chayta", which would mean, offering or gift.

The apus, the sacred mountains

The apus is the name given to the sacred mountains. But it would be necessary to understand why the Incas worshipped their apus, and why the current people of these times, especially in the Andes Mountains, continue to worship the apus.

In our concept, it is very easy to understand, if one is a farmer, who grows corn, potatoes, or any agricultural product, he needs the element of water. The same if you are a shepherd, you need better pastures for your animals (llamas, alpacas, nowadays cows, sheep, horses), and you need the element water. It is a simple rule, if there is no water, there is no life.

Now it is understood when the Incas worshiped the mountains with snow as the apu Ausangate[4], the apu Salkantay, the apu Wakay Willka, or Veronica, and many others. Why from them constantly descends the water element.

The question would be: Why did the Incas worship the mountains, knowing that in the Andes there are hundreds or thousands of mountains? Because in some mountains, not in all of them, there are waterfalls, water springs, lakes, lagoons, large rivers, or small rivers. We come to the same conclusion: it is the water element. But, at the same time, when the apus provide you with water, in the rainy season, these can cause thaws and avalanches. These produce, as a whole, overflows of lakes, lagoons, causing landslides or rocks, destroying in its path from the highlands to the valleys, villages, bridges, roads, and causing human beings a great tragedy. Thus, the apus can be generous but, at the same time, they can cause many misfortunes.

This veneration to the apus, was perhaps a tradition that was practiced since pre- Inca times. It has continued to this day, especially in the city of Cusco. Like the Pachamama, offerings are made to them, being coca, *mullu*, corn, fetus, llama, or alpaca bait as the

---

4   This glacier can be observed when trekking the Siete Colores mountain

CHAPTER IV: THE RELIGION OF THE INCAS

most appreciated offerings. When one makes the Inca Trail to the citadel of Machu Picchu, you can see in its path, from the beginning to the end, a large number of apus, which can be observed in the Inca Trail to Machu Picchu.

This is the religious system that the Incas practiced until before the arrival of the Spaniards. It was a religion in contact with nature. Their natural phenomena and their visible gods such as the sun, the moon, the stars, the lightning, the thunder, the rainbow, the love for Mother Nature, and their sacred mountains.

The huacas

The huacas in Inca times were sacred places or objects such as religious constructions, a mountain, a lake, a lagoon, a river, a stream, a cave, a tree, a stone, an idol, a mummy, etc., any place, natural or human, considered sacred by the Incas.

The huacas were protective spirits, which manifested themselves in different ways. The

Adoration of the Huacas. Drawing by Felipe Guaman Poma de Ayala, "Nueva Coronica y Buen Gobierno", 1615..

Incas believed that some people, such as the Sapa Inca and the priests, had the power to speak with these supernatural powers. Through them, they could know the facts of the past or the future, as well as ask them for good prosperity, especially in **the sowing** season on the part of the peasants. The same was done by shepherds who asked for their animals to multiply.

While the huacas were worshiped, if they did not fulfill the task of protection or did not have good omens, they were punished. Thus, when the Incas conquered towns or lordships, the local huacas of the conquered were taken to Cusco, where they were venerated. But, at the same time, they were taken as hostages, if the local chiefs or curacas did not follow the rules of the Empire. These huacas could be destroyed, thus erasing the connection between the conquered peoples and their local gods.

These huacas exist to this day throughout the Peruvian Andes, in the coastal, highland, and jungle regions, and are still venerated. In colonial times, the Spanish destroyed many huacas to build on top of them a Catholic temple or placed the image of a cross. There are several examples of these in the city of Cusco, such as the Huaca of Tetecaca and the Catholic temples around the Plaza de Armas which, in Inca times, were ceremonial places and today are Catholic temples.

The mallquis, the mummies

The mallquis were the mummies. In the Inca period, they were the object of cults because it was believed that the death of a human being was only a passage to another life. No one was afraid of it, since their descendants, relatives, and loved ones would take care of them, giving them offerings and ceremonies. This religious practice continues today. Every year, on November 2nd, the Day of the Dead is celebrated, where people visit the cementeries, bringing them food, music, and flowers. On this occasion, a small party is held, reminding them that these dead, or *mallquis*, are still in our minds and hearts.

CHAPTER IV: THE RELIGION OF THE INCAS

In Inca times, people belonging to the upper class were mummified in a fetal position, which was placed in altars to be venerated, as when the Spaniards arrived at Q'oricancha, they saw inside the important temples, the mallquis of the Sapa Incas. The common people were buried in cemeteries as well in a fetal position, with their personal objects. But, in several cases, they were placed in mountain caves, as can be seen in the archaeological complex of Pisac or in the findings made by Hiram Bingham when he discovered the Inca city of Machu Picchu.

Adoration to the mallquis. Drawing by Felipe Guaman Poma de Ayala, "Nueva Coronica y Buen Gobierno", 1615.

THE INCA TRAIL TO MACHU PICCHU

CHAPTER V
THE SOCIAL ORGANIZATION OF THE INCAS

The social organization of the Incas was based on a hierarchical system of political, economic, and religious domination, where the Sapa Inca was considered the supreme person, "Son of the Sun", therefore a god come true who could be seen as the Sun God. This organization is as the historian Waldemar Espinoza Soriano states:

> "It was a class society, with strongly closed classes, with different statuses and rights conditioned by family and ethnic descent. This determined wealth, occupation or trade, clothing, ornaments, and daily life. They formed exclusive and permanent groups with insurmountable social barriers, with differentiated economic activities. However, the strict dissimilarity was not racial but economic and social. Each group had rights, obligations, and privileges; each had its myths and mythical and magical symbolism; its members were subject to taboos or prohibitions. Class and caste were inherited. However, the merits of individuals of the lower strata were recognized. Thus, strategists, valiant warriors, skillful craftsmen and soothsayers who were not mistaken enjoyed prestige; but the merits of the progenitors were not trans-

mitted to the children, although the latter could feel proud of their parents"[5].

In this social organization the Sapa Inca was the highest authority and the ayllu, agriculture being the fundamental basis of its economy and in regular or small percentage especially in the highlands above 4,000 meters above sea level throughout the Andes the breeding of camelids (llama, alpaca) especially.

The Sapa Inca

The term Sapa Inca referred to the emperor at the time of Tawantinsuyo. For us, today, we will call him Inca, to understand it better. The Inca was the highest political, economic, social, military, and religious authority of the Inca Empire:

1. Politically, he was the one who regulated the political base

Mural fresco by Juan Bravo. Detail of the social organization of the Incas, Cusco, June 1992.

---

5   Waldemar Espinoza Soriano, "LOS INCAS, economía sociedad y estado en la era del Tahuantinsuyo", 1997 Pag. 296.

CHAPTER V: THE SOCIAL ORGANIZATION OF THE INCAS

regional or local governors of the towns or cities, who had to report periodically on their work.
2. Economically, the Inca was the one who distributed farmland to all social classes, and it was the Inca who owned the largest amount of farmland in the entire territory.
3. In military matters, he was the one who appointed the army commanders, who had to be loyal to the Inca. He was in command of the army to conquer local towns or ethnic groups.
4. In religious matters, he was the one who ordered the religious system that the people had to follow, especially after the government of Pachacúteq, where the Sun God was the supreme god. He was the one who directed the religious ceremonies because he was considered the intermediary between the gods and human beings. The origin of the Inca was considered divine since he descended from the Sun god. He was a real god who could be seen. This happened from the government of the Inca Pachacúteq who regulated the religious system, being the major god of the Inca State the Sun.

The Inca had as his main wife his sister, the *Coya*, to maintain the power caste or to maintain the royal blood. However, at the same time, he had a harem of noblewomen or concubines, belonging to other ayllus, or families, and ethnic groups, this with the idea of creating family ties and political power. In general, the Inca nobility is divided into several classes.

Nobility of blood

The nobility of blood, constituted by the whole family environment of the blood of the Inca, among which we have:

1. The Coya was the main wife of the Inca, who was one of his sisters, to maintain the purity of the royal family.
2. The *Auqui* was the beloved son of the Inca, who would be designated as the future Inca. Very different from European cultures, where the firstborn son (the first son) was appointed as the new king. In Inca times, before the arrival of the Spaniards, many Incas were chosen by the royal panacas (family lineages), where women played a very important role.
3. The Ñusta was the daughter or daughters of the Inca.

The nobility of upstarts

This social class was made up of the rulers or chiefs of the conquered towns, lordships, and kingdoms, who had been peacefully subdued. To maintain their privileges they had to be loyal to the Empire, which was embodied in the Inca as supreme ruler.

The nobility of privilege

This social class was made up of those people who for their achievements: wars, construction of public, state, religious and other works in favor of the State. They had achieved the liking of the Inca and could rise to the next social rank.

In this social class of the nobility are the famous *orejones* or *big ears*, who as children were fitted with a metal disc and when they reached adulthood they wore as earrings some metal discs, in gold, silver and copper, which gave them a rank of power. These "orejones" also had short hair as a sign of social status.

In this social class, we must also consider the religious apparatus where one of the brothers of the Inca was the high priest, called *Willaq Uma*. Sometimes in the absence of the Sapa Inca, it was the Willaq Uma who took command of the power of the Empire. He was also the one who took the maskaypacha to name the new Inca. Thus, in Inca times, the priestly class had great participation in the government of each ruler.

The people
The town was divided into different social classes:
1. The *hatun runas* were the majority population of the Tawantinsuyo, who carried out agricultural, livestock, handicraft, public, state, and religious works. They paid tribute to the Empire under a labor tax (labor). They could also serve the Inca army. They lived grouped under the ayllu system.
2. The *mitimaes* were groups of families in charge of populating, colonizing, teaching, educating, and disseminating the conquered peoples or territories and enforcing economic, political, and religious functions.
3. The *acllas* were the chosen women, who were brought from different towns or territories at the age of 8 or 10 years old to serve the Inca or the Sun God. They lived in the *acllawasis* (*aclla*, chosen and *wasi*, house) or "House of the Chosen Women", where they were prepared to perform domestic tasks such as preparing food, preparing the girl, making clothes, and performing religious activities, under the supervision of the *mamaconas*, or older women, who were highly respected in Inca times.
4. The *yanaconas* were those people of the conquered peoples or ethnic groups, who had lost all their rights. They were considered servants for life, maintaining their status generation after generation. They performed all **kinds of work, from domestic tasks, such as housekeeping, to agriculture and livestock.**
5. The *pinas* or *piñas* were those prisoners of the conquered peoples who did not accept that they had been conquered

by the Incas, maintaining their disobedience to the Inca government, for which they were transferred especially to the jungle territories, difficult places to live, because of the living conditions, in addition to the climate, mosquitoes, snakes, and others. Also, they were those people who were dedicated to the work of planting and harvesting coca leaves, the same that was inherited from one generation to another.

Unlike in the ancient cultures of the Old World, where slaves were considered objects of commerce and could be bought or sold, in Inca times, slaves were not bought or sold.

PART TWO

THE INCA TRAIL TO MACHU PICCHU

THE INCA TRAIL TO MACHU PICCHU

CHAPTER VI
THE INCA ROADS

When we speak of the Inca roads before the Spanish invasion, we must first establish the limits of this immense territory that was once Tawantinsuyo. The "empire of the four regions" extended through the Andes from Colombia and Ecuador, passing through Bolivia, Argentina, Chile, and of course Peru.

Our planet earth, in its five continents, has more than 185 ecological levels. The Peruvian territory has more than 85 of these floors, from the Peruvian sea (zero levels), through the coastal valleys, the Andean valleys, the mountains that pass over 6,000 meters above sea level, reaching the Amazon jungle. Each ecological floor has its flora, fauna, geography, and rocks, which provided the Inca inhabitants with the material resources for the construction of their llaqtas (cities), ceremonial sites, tampus (resting places), qollqas (deposits), pukaras (guard and control posts), cultivation platforms, bridges, and roads.

The development of the Tawantinsuyo took place in very rugged territory. The Inca ethnic group, in its expansion process, covered large territories that were given special importance when defeating the Chancas. The conquest of the Pacific coast, by the dominion of the Chinchas (great fishermen and navigators), allowed the Incas, in the time of Pachacúteq, to extend the limits of the empire to the maximum towards the west. At the same time, the "Sons of the Sun" also extended their territory southward to the Lake Titicaca region. Later, Pachacúteq's successors continued this process of conquest until Huayna Cápac, who reached the territories of the current countries of Ecuador and Colombia, and to the south with the territories of the countries of Chile and Argentina.

To manage and control their space, the Incas built thousands of kilometers of roads throughout their territory. Many of these roads were reused by the Incas, since before them, local people built their roads to link their territories to transport their agricultural resources (corn, potatoes, coca, and others), as well as to move their animals (llamas, alpacas) and their armies.

Before the arrival of the Incas, the Qotakallis, the Lucres, and the Killkis built important roads to link the Vilcanota valley. And the Waris, who came in their advance from Ayacucho to Cusco, crossed the Apurimac territories building their roads.

The Qhapaq Ñan

This network of roads is called the Qhapaq Ñan. It is the oldest road system in South America, crossing large territories in the Andes mountain range, from the Pacific coast to the Amazon, passing through the current countries of Colombia, Ecuador, Peru, Bolivia, Chile, and Argentina.

The Qhapaq Ñan was the backbone of the power of the Incas, linked as a set of bridle paths, stairways, bridges, water canals, resting places, ceremonial centers, villages, and large cities. A very clear example is the Inca road to the citadel of Machu Picchu, which had as its starting point the most important temple of the Inca Empire: the Q'oricancha.

CHAPTER VI: THE INCA ROADS

From the temple of the Sun, all the roads of the Empire departed through a system of huacas and *ceques*, which was a network of imaginary roads in a straight line. At a certain distance, there was a ceremonial place.

As we have already mentioned, the Tawantinsuyo was divided into four main regions. From the Q'oricancha, four main roads departed from Cusco to these large territories, which were connected to smaller towns and valleys through secondary connections. These routes, in turn, must have had small branches, which connected with ceremonial sites, farmlands, llama, and alpaca grazing areas.

The roads integrated the entire Inca State from north to south and from east to west, comprising four main routes:
1. From Cusco, Peru, to Quito, Ecuador, with a branch to Pasto, Colombia.
2. From Cusco to Nazca and the city of Ica (where the famous giant lines are located) and to Tumbes, a border city between Peru and Ecuador.
3. From Cusco to Chuquiago, in Bolivia, near La Paz.
4. Finally, from Cusco to Arica and Atacama in Chile, with a branch to the Maule River in Argentina, near the city of Tucumán.

The Qhapaq Ñan probably had an extension of more than 25,000 kilometers[6], which varied in width from one meter to more than six meters, especially in the coastal zone and the wide valleys.

In the regions of Contisuyo and Chinchaysuyo (today the entire Peruvian coast) the Inca roads were marked by stones from the sea since it is a flat and sandy territory, where it is very easy to get lost. They placed tree trunks in certain places, to show the

---
[6] 16,630 miles.

traveler the way to follow. The same thing happens today in the mountains. If someone does not know the true path to follow, he can easily get lost, since llamas and alpacas make many paths. At the time of the Inca Empire, the Incas must have built at a certain distance earth or stone mounds to follow the right path. And in the jungle, they probably painted some rocks to point out the right way.

These roads vary in their type of construction, due to the relief of the Andes mountain range, flat or undulating. On the roads going up and down, the Incas built steps or stairways made of stone. And to protect them, especially during the rainy season, they built water channels to link territories. In some cases, the Incas built bridges, small, short, or long, to cross rivers.

The construction of small bridges required flat blocks of stone. However, for medium-sized bridges, the Incas used tree trunks (alder, queña, chachacomo). The floor was made of tree branches and the upper part was filled with *champas*, or blocks of earth and grass, which provided a comfortable place to cross.

In places where there were large rivers, to connect villages, the Incas built suspension bridges, made with ichu, but this already included a large number of people. Today, the famous Queswar Chaka bridge, located in the province of Canas, still exists three hours from Cusco. Year after year it is rebuilt by the local villages in a festive atmosphere, as it serves to unite the towns.

The Peruvian Government, with the idea of rescuing and putting in value the pre- Hispanic Inca roads, has created through its Ministry of Culture, an organization called *Qhapaq Ñan Project*. The main task of this organization is to locate, study, restore and enhance the value of these roads and consequently protect them, which is why on June 25, 2014, at the 38th Conference of UNESCO agencies, held in Doha (Qatar), it was added to the list of World Heritage in the area of Education, Science and Culture.

The Inca Trail to Machu Picchu and its regulation

The famous "Inca Trail to Machu Picchu" is located within the Historic Sanctuary of Machu Picchu. It was created by Supreme Decree N° 001-81-AA, issued by the Peruvian Government. The Machu Picchu Historic Sanctuary is a protected area covering a territory of 32,592 hectares, located in the district of Machu Picchu, province of Urubamba in the department of Cusco. It comprises the natural and cultural, the environment of the Inca city of Machu Picchu, nestled in the Peruvian Andes, on the banks of the Urubamba River that runs northwest. Having as objectives:

1. Protect the Inca citadel of Machu Picchu and the group of archaeological groups, which are connected by the Qhapaq Ñan, as tangible heritage.
2. To conserve the landscape environment, the natural habitat of flora and fauna, and those that are vulnerable to extinction.

The Historic Sanctuary of Machu Picchu

The Historic Sanctuary of Machu Picchu (SHMP) is geographically located in the middle of the great Urubamba River and around two mountain ranges, the Urubamba and Vilcabamba ranges, with the highest snow-capped peaks, the Veronica (Wakay Willka), and the Salkantay, as well as the Urubamba, Aobamba and Cusichaca valleys.

The SHMP has registered several well-defined zones, being the most relevant from the ecological point of view the high Andean grasslands, the high altitude dwarf forests, and the high jungle or yungas, represented by the cloud forests, with a variety of ecological floors in terms of flora and fauna, being a very surprising place.

The Inca Trail to the city of Machu Picchu has been regulated by the representative entities of the Peruvian State such as the Ministry of Culture, SERNANP (Ministry of Environment), and DIRCETUR (Ministry of Tourism).

In 1995, Supreme Decree N° 26 - 95 - ITINCI was published in the *Peruvian newspaper El Peruano*, with the Regulations for tourist use and conservation of natural resources on the Inca Trail within the Machu Picchu Historic Sanctuary. This regulation was signed by the then President of the Republic, Alberto Fujimori, the Minister of Industry, Tourism, Integration and International Trade Negotiations, Liliana Canales Novella, and the Minister of Agriculture, Absalón Vásquez Villanueva. This regulation came into force in 1996.

The main objective of this regulation is to promote and contribute to the conservation of the cultural and natural heritage of Machu Picchu, with a rule for the use of the Inca Trail, to reduce the impacts caused by visitors and ensure their safety.

According to this regulation, the Inca Trail can only be done in organized groups under the direction of an authorized official tour guide. Each organized group must have logistical support, porters (local people) authorized to do the Inca Trail, who will be in charge of carrying all the trekking equipment (personal tents, kitchen tent, dining tent, bathroom tent, tables, benches, kitchenware), provisions, and the garbage that will be collected for the days of the trek.

Being the maximum number of people in a group of 45 people: 16 passengers and 29 logistic people (guides, cooks, and porters). All organized groups must have the *authorization* of a travel agency that has an operating permit and is accredited by DIRCETUR and the Technical Management of Machu Picchu.

CHAPTER VI: THE INCA ROADS

The Inca Trail to Machu Picchu can be done from March 1st to January 31st. Except for February, when the Inca Trail is closed for maintenance, recovery of local flora and fauna, and safety reasons due to the rainy season.

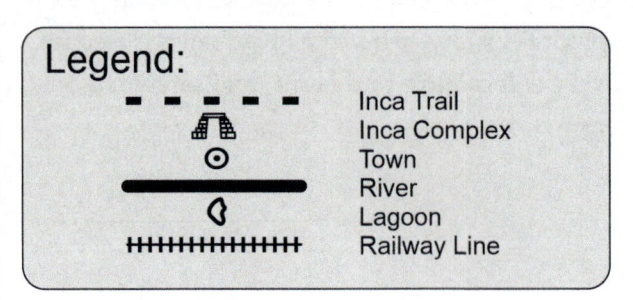

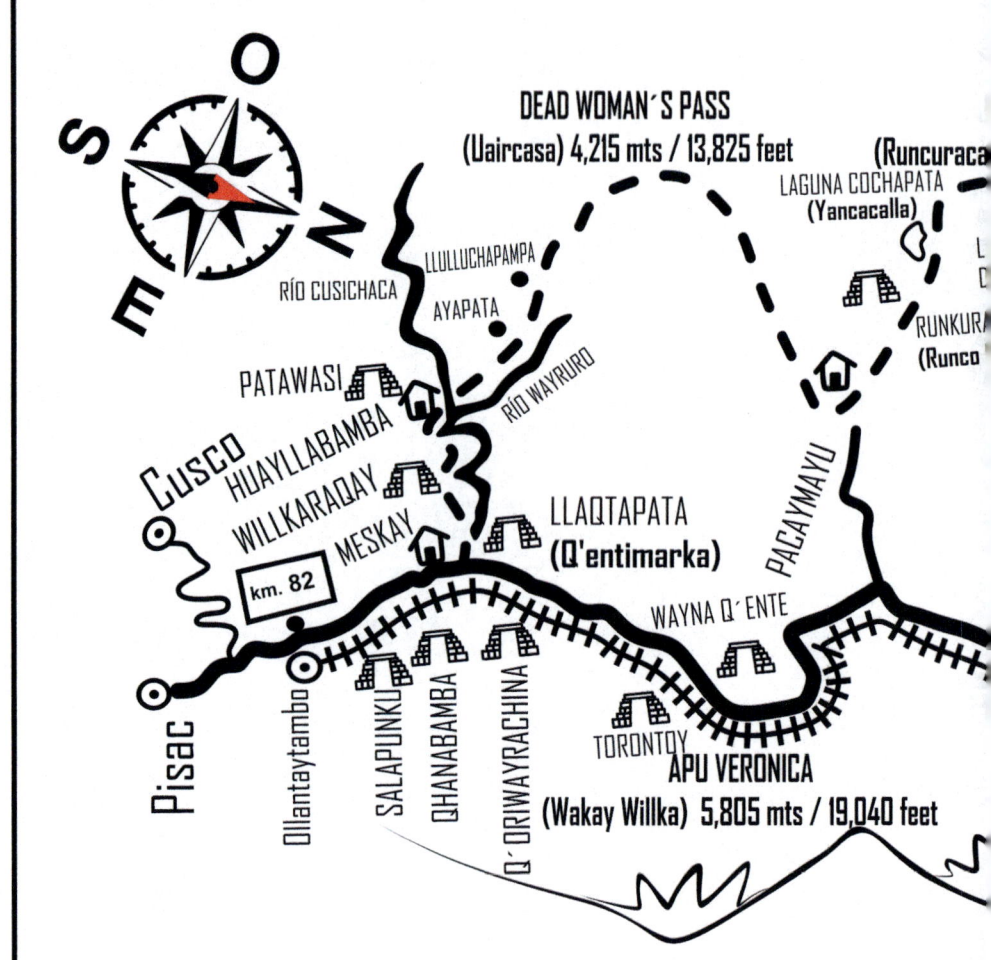

THE INCA TRAIL TO MACHU PICCHU

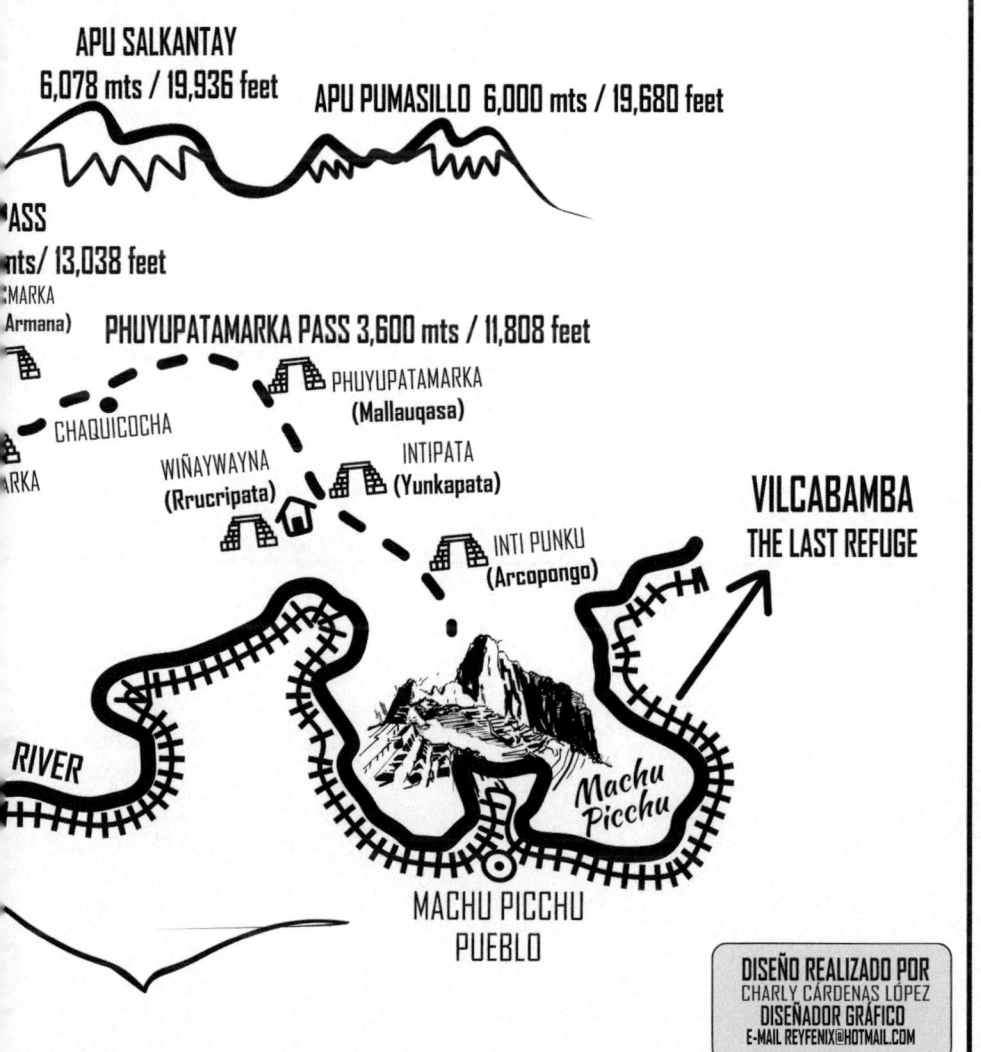

IL TO MACHU PICCHU
DAYS / 3 NIGHTS

APU SALKANTAY 6,078 mts / 19,936 feet

APU PUMASILLO 6,000 mts / 19,680 feet

ASS
mts / 13,038 feet

MARKA
(Armana)

PHUYUPATAMARKA PASS 3,600 mts / 11,808 feet

CHAQUICOCHA

PHUYUPATAMARKA (Mallauqasa)

WIÑAYWAYNA (Rrucripata)

INTIPATA (Yunkapata)

INTI PUNKU (Arcopongo)

VILCABAMBA THE LAST REFUGE

RIVER

Machu Picchu

MACHU PICCHU PUEBLO

DISEÑO REALIZADO POR
CHARLY CÁRDENAS LÓPEZ
DISEÑADOR GRÁFICO
E-MAIL REYFENIX@HOTMAIL.COM

THE INCA TRAIL TO MACHU PICCHU

CHAPTER VII
THE TRADITIONAL INCA TRAIL TO MACHU PICCHU (4 DAYS AND 3 NIGHTS)

Today, the Inca Trail is famous because it includes in its route -which is done for 5, 4, or 2 days- a great variety of ecological levels. These include a great diversity of flora and fauna, from the low area near the Urubamba River, where the town of Aguas Calientes is located, at 2,000 meters/6,560 feet above sea level, to the high area, whose high point is the Warmiwañuska Pass, or Dead Woman's Pass, at 4,215 meters/13,825 feet altitude.

You can appreciate its wildlife, such as the *ukuku*, or spectacled bear, deer, foxes and the majestic *kuntur*, or Andean condor. In addition to this, the landscapes of the valleys, with mountains over 6,000 meters high, and the incredible views are shown as living paintings. Along with the Inca constructions made by a culture that had great respect for nature that the local people call "love for the Pachamama".

The Inca Trail includes not only the spirit of adventure, personal challenge, a dream, but also its history. The history of a great culture that existed before the arrival of the Spaniards in South America, with its religion, customs, ways of life, beliefs, food, etc. that persist to this day.

This trail, from its starting point to the final destination, the Inca city of Machu Picchu, offers a large number of ceremonial centers. These are located in strategic places from where you can observe the tutelary gods of the Incas and the apus, such as the Salkantay, the Veronica, and the Pumasillo. Arriving at the Inca citadel, one can understand why the Incas built this iconic site, in the middle of two mountains: Machu Picchu and Huayna Picchu.

Bordering Machu Picchu and the Huayna Picchu mountain, is the Willkamayu, or Urubamba River.

The Inca Trail to Machu Picchu

The Inca Trail to Machu Picchu, today, starts at kilometer 82, also called Piscacucho village. This route is one of the most famous hikes in the Cusco area because in its route you have a great variety

Piscacucho or Km. 82, the starting point of the Inca Trail.

CHAPTER VII: THE TRADITIONAL INCA TRAIL TO MACHU PICCHU (4 DAYS-3 NIGHTS)

of Inca sites, which were in Inca times agricultural centers, warehouses, resting places, checkpoints, ceremonial centers, villages, to the end of this route to reach the famous Inca llaqta.

Besides, there is a great variety of ecosystems with flora and fauna typical of the area, its landscapes, glaciers, mountains, lagoons, rivers, waterfalls, and a variety of climates throughout the year.

On the first day, before starting this hike, you can observe the largest river in Cusco: the Willkamayu, or Urubamba River, which changes its flow according to the time of year.

Crossing the bridge, this great adventure to Machu Picchu begins. Thus, on the first day of the tour, you will be able to observe from a distance the archaeological complexes of Salapunku, Qhanabamba, and LLaqtapata. But you can also visit the complex of Willkaraqay, passing through some small villages such as Karpamayu, Meskay, and Hatun Chaka, too, at the end of the day, arrive at the first camp called Huayllabamba.

On the second day, the Inca trail is more scenic and personally challenging, having to reach the highest point of this trek: the "Paso de la Mujer Muerta" (Dead Woman's Pass). The journey from the first camp in Huayllabamba (3,000 meters/9,840 feet) is upward, where there is a great variety of ecological levels, highlighting the local flora and fauna. In addition to this, there are landscapes with incredible views. And when you reach the highest point, you descend to the second camp of Pacaymayu, a cobblestone road.

The third day will be the most interesting because you will be able to visit Inca complexes. The first place to visit will be Runkuraqay, from where you can observe the Pacaymayu valley and the Warmiwañuska Pass. Then comes the site of Sayacmarka, which has an incredible view of the Vilcabamba mountain range, where two important apus, the Salkantay and Pumasillo, stand out.

THE INCA TRAIL TO MACHU PICCHU

Another magnificent site will be Qonchamarka. From this point, the hike becomes simpler, with small ascents and descents, to reach the Phuyupatamarka pass. From this place, you can see the Urubamba valley, the apu Veronica, the archaeological complex of Intipata, the mountain of Machu Picchu, and behind it, the famous citadel.

From the Phuyupatamarka pass, we descend to the last camp of Wiñaywayna. On the way, we visit the archaeological complexes of Phuyupatamarka, Intipata, and Wiñaywayna.

On the fourth day, after much physical and mental effort, we arrive at the famous Intipunku, from where you can see Machu Picchu with the famous Huayna Picchu mountain. Surrounding the Inca citadel is the sacred river of Willkamayu, and then descend to the ancient city. As you descend, the hiker will understand that the Inca Trail to Machu Picchu is a challenge accomplished.

The apu Veronica, or Wakay Willka. Sacred mountain in the sacred valley of the Incas.

CHAPTER VII: THE TRADITIONAL INCA TRAIL TO MACHU PICCHU (4 DAYS-3 NIGHTS)

As a mountain guide, with more than 25 years of experience, I would like to share with you this unique adventure, to feel the energy of the Andes, the love for the Pachamama and the Apus. And at the end of this journey feel this life experience that can be shared with family and friends.

The classic Inca Trail to Machu Picchu is 4 days and 3 nights. However, it can also be done in 5 days and 4 nights. In this case, we will do the classic route in 4 days and 3 nights.

Day 1 - Training day

To make this famous trekking, most travel agencies organize the departure time from the city of Cusco to the starting point of the Inca trail, near the town of Piscacucho or "kilometer 82", at 6.00 am. This trip takes approximately three hours. From the city of Cusco to the town of Ollantaytambo, it takes approximately two hours, and from Ollantaytambo to the starting point, it takes about fifty minutes. On the way, there is a thirty-minute stop in the town of Ollantaytambo to have breakfast or make some purchases such as trekking poles, rain ponchos, snacks, and other items.

Some travel agencies include breakfast on the first day and others do not. But, in the last year, many hotels and hostels provide a small "box breakfast" as part of the service.

The recommendation I would give is to leave Cusco early: at 5:00 a.m. Why? Because when leaving Cusco early, the trekker will be one of the first people to pass the first checkpoint, especially in May, June, July, and August, which is considered the high season. This checkpoint sometimes takes more than an hour. The park rangers take a long time in their control task, verifying if the passport number coincides with the number you have on the Inca Trail permit and your nationality.

If you want to enjoy this hike, the biggest tip is very simple: get up early. The hiker will be able to enjoy the hike without haste, take time for photos, observe the local fauna and flora and enjoy the explanations of the mountain guides.

After passing the first checkpoint, the hiker crosses a large bridge where you can see one of the largest rivers near the city of Cusco: the Willkamayu River (from *willka*; sacred and *mayu*; river). In colonial times, the Spaniards changed its name to the Urubamba River. During the dry season, from May to October, this river is calm, but during the rainy season, from December to April, it is quite abundant. The river accompanies the hiker for the first two hours. After this, you will take another path through the Cusichaca valley. On the third day, the Urubamba River will be observed again when descending to the last camp called Wiñaywayna.

Crossing the bridge, approximately 15 minutes, there is a small house on the right side of the road. It is a place where you can take a short break. If you turn around, you will see in front of you the majestic mountain, called by the local people the Apu Wakay Willka, which was changed, in colonial times, by the Catholic name Veronica. Why Veronica? When the Spaniards were in the process of evangelizing the Inca settlers, they changed the name of the Apu Wakay Willka to Veronica because of the shape of this mountain with a head and outstretched arms.

According to Spanish bullfighting customs, Veronica is a throw that is made by holding the cape with both hands in front of the bull. And according to the Catholic Gospels, it was Veronica who

CHAPTER VII: THE TRADITIONAL INCA TRAIL TO MACHU PICCHU (4 DAYS-3 NIGHTS)

wiped the face of Jesus of Nazareth, when he was about to be crucified.

Veronica is observed throughout the Inca trail until reaching the city of Machu Picchu. It has a cardinal east orientation, that is, towards sunrise. This can be verified using a compass.

Following the trail, from the first resting place, about fifteen minutes to the right side is the second house, where a family offers the service of bathrooms and where you can buy drinks. If the hiker asks the owner of the house kindly about crossing her house, he will see at the other end of the valley the first archaeological site called Salapunku. Many guides do not take tourists to observe this very interesting Inca complex. Another archaeological site, Salapunku, is at the other end of the Urubamba River.

Salapunku

The archaeological site of Salapunku, is located at km 83 of the railway line between Cusco and Aguas Calientes Pueblo, on the right bank of the Urubamba River. Located in the district of Machu Picchu, province of Urubamba, its UTM coordinates are:

East	North	Altitude (masl and feet)
782617.2	782617.2	2,638/8,653

For José Gabriel Cosio (1920), Salapunku would mean "room", stone fragments for fortresses, and "punku", door. Salapunku is a doorway that would serve as access to another enclosure or smaller room as the main part of the complex, from which the place is named.

There is not much ethnographic information about this place. It is only known that it would be within the private property

The archaeological complex of Salapunku is located at the right end of the Urubamba River.

of the Inca Pachacúteq. The ethnohistoric information refers to the location of "Picchu" on the Chaullay bridge and the documentary identification of Q'enti Marka and other lands along the Urubamba River, which belonged to the ninth Inca. This would also include the lands of Cedrobamba and the Inca trail to Machu Picchu.

In 1911, when the American explorer Hiram Bingham was exploring the location of the Inca city of Vilcabamba (last refuge of the Incas), he made a base camp in this place. He must have made some explorations to identify this archaeological site and located a large water channel that came from the heights of Choquelluska, passing through the lower part of the Veronica hill, until it reached the archaeological site of Qhanabamba.

In the archaeological works carried out by the English archaeologist Ana Kendall in 1992, circular and ovoid constructions were found, associated with Killki style ceramics, which would belong to the period of the regional states (Late Intermediate). That is to say that Salapunku would have been occupied before by the Killki regional state, which advanced from the Cusco valley to the Vilcanota valley, in search of better fields for planting corn, having to build a road at the same time, which was reused in the Inca period, in the process of advancing towards the Antisuyo region (high jungle).

The research work carried out by archaeologist Francisco Huarcaya, under the supervision of the Ministry of Culture of Cusco, in 2008, in his *"Annual Research Report on the Salapunku Archaeological Ensemble"*, states that the site was in the process of construction at the time it was abandoned since a large number of tools such as strikers, hammers and lithic polishers were found.

THE INCA TRAIL TO MACHU PICCHU

> Salapunku must have been a ceremonial and administrative center of the entrance to the ntisuyo.

Salapunku must have been a very important ceremonial and administrative center of entry to the high jungle, where the city of Machu Picchu is located. There are also open spaces, which would have been intended to house even a large number of people, as well as several *kallankas*, or very large rectangular constructions. In our modern times, they would be like the famous "backpacker hostels". There is also a small huaca that resembles the apu Veronica in shape with an orientation to the east, giving it its religious and sacred character.

At the top of the so-called "gate," there is a sequence of zigzagging cyclopean walls, similar to those seen in the archaeological complex of Sacsayhuaman, which would represent the god Illapa.

The type of architecture in Salapunku is very varied, ranging from the use of large stones, or cyclopean, to small stones, of a

CHAPTER VII: THE TRADITIONAL INCA TRAIL TO MACHU PICCHU (4 DAYS-3 NIGHTS)

simple carving, joined with mud mortar, except for the sector called the gate, which has a more detailed and fine work.

Continuing with our tour, thirty-five or forty minutes from the Salapunku sector, we will arrive at a small resting place from where we will be able to observe the archaeological site of Qhanabamba.

Qhanabamba

Qhanabamba is located approximately 500 meters from Salapunku, on the right bank of the Urubamba River, in a northeasterly direction. Its UTM coordinates are:

East	North	Altitude (masl and ffeet)
780990.6	8536065.7	2,603/8,538

The type of construction that is presented in the Inca complex of Qhanabamba, are rectangular enclosures, of regular size. The architecture is very simple, with blocks of stones of regular and

The archaeological complex of Qhanabamba, also called Ninamarka

small sizes, joined with mud mortar. These constructions must have had very simple roofs, with tree trunks, branches, and thatched roofs. Due to its location around the Urubamba valley, Qhanabamba must have been a tampu, or resting place, in the direction of Machu Picchu, since there is an Inca trail that runs along the Urubamba valley.

Very close to this complex, there are four circular constructions of simple architecture, which must have been qollqas, or warehouses, to store food, weapons, or other items for travelers on their way to Machu Picchu.

In colonial times, Qhanabamba, may have been burned by the Inca settlers, in their escape to the last refuge, called Vilcabamba. Perhaps this is the origin of the name Qhanabamba, from *qhana*, to burn, and *bamba*, town. Some local archaeologists mention that the site must have had another name in Inca times, Ninamarka,

Qhanabamba, must have been a tampu, or resting place.

CHAPTER VII: THE TRADITIONAL INCA TRAIL TO MACHU PICCHU (4 DAYS-3 NIGHTS)

View over the Urubamba valley, with its main river, the Willkamayu.

from *nina*, fire and *marka*, village. Perhaps, after this construction was burned, the place was abandoned by the Incas.

It is important to mention that this area flows the water channel that comes from the Choquelluska sector. It passes through the Salapunku complex. Very close to Qhanabamba there is an extensive flat area, which must have been used in Inca times for the cultivation of corn, the same that is still used today by a local family.

After 25 minutes of walking, we begin to ascend to reach the village of Meskay. It is a very small village, whose inhabitants are peasants who grow corn and potatoes only for family sustenance. In this place, the hiker can take a break, use the restrooms (1 sol), buy drinks such as water, and have the opportunity to drink the local drink: chicha. It is fermented corn. In Inca times, chicha was a sacred drink for human consumption.

Meskay village, where the hiker can buy drinks and "snacks".

Continuing our adventure, we will take the path of a small valley, and then ascend to a viewpoint, from where we can observe the apu, Veronica. After about five minutes, we will arrive at a great viewpoint, from where we will observe the archaeological complex of Llaqtapata, today called Q'entimarka, from *q'enti*, hummingbird, and *marka*, village. This may be due to the presence of many hummingbirds during the rainy season. Very close to this viewpoint is the site of Willkaraqay.

Wllkaraqay

The archaeological site of Willkaray is located in the upper part of Llaqtapata, on a landslide of rocks and earth that must have happened thousands of years ago, on a high point from where

CHAPTER VII: THE TRADITIONAL INCA TRAIL TO MACHU PICCHU (4 DAYS-3 NIGHTS)

you can see a section of the Cusichaca valley and the Apu Veronica, having a panoramic view.

Willkaraqay is located on the right bank of the Cusichaca River and less than a kilometer on the left bank of the Urubamba River. This Inca complex is in the district of Ollantaytambo, province of Urubamba, and its UTM coordinates are:

East	North	Altitude (masl and feet)
779266.6	8535407	2,745/9,004

Its boundaries are, to the north, the rural community of Chamana; to the south, the mountain and the Leonniyoc ravine; to the east, the Trankapata site and the Walanqay river; and to the west, Aqo Q'asa and the Cusichaca river, from *cusi*, happy and *chaca*, bridge.

The archaeological complex of Willkaraqay, a ceremonial and dwelling center.

In 2003, the archaeologist Richard Alegria Sanchez, in his *"annual report of Archaeological Research in the Archaeological Ensemble of Willkaraqay, Sector "A" and "B"*, states to have found in his archaeological findings, ceramic fragments of Inca style, Killki and Formative period. This is important because it shows us that this place would have been occupied earlier by a regional state of the Cusco valley, continuing with its stage of territorial expansion in search of better land for growing corn. At the same time, they had to build a road to connect this place, which must have been reused in the Inca period.

Willkaraqay has two platforms that archaeologists have divided as "sector A" and "sector B":

Sector A would be occupied by buildings of rectangular shapes, with open doors. Inside there are niches, or false windows, trapezoidal in shape, which must have had a thatched roof in Inca times, also having a small open square, facing west towards the Cusichaca River and the archaeological site of Llaqtapata.

In sector B, there are rectangular constructions. Inside are niches, which must have served as homes for a very important class of people. It should be noted that very close to Willkaraqay there is a group of enclosures that have the same characteristics of sector B, which must have served as housing.

As for the type of architecture in this place, it is from the pre-Inca (Killkis) and Incas. They used this promontory of land to make their constructions, using the materials available in the area: carved stones, river stones, possibly brought from the Cusichaca or Urubamba rivers, joined with mud mortar. Very close to this place, there are clay mines that could have been used for the preparation of the mud mortar.

Willkaraqay would be part of the archaeological site of Llaqtapata, due to its proximity and location. It must have been in the Inca period a single village but divided into two sectors, if we keep the Inca tradition, those of the Hanan and Hurin.

Llaqtapata (Q'entimarka)

The archaeological site of Llaqtapata is located on the left bank of the Urubamba River, between the slopes of the Casamentuyoc hill and the Cusichaca River, a tributary of the Urubamba River. The orientation of the Inca city is oriented towards the east (sunrise) and the apu Veronica. Its UTM coordinates are:

East	North	Altitude (masl and feet)
779091	8535900.8	2,600/8,528

The archaeological complex of Llaqtapata, called in Inca times as Q'entimarka.

This site has several names: Patallaqta was given by the American explorer Hiram Bingham; and in current times, the Ministry of Culture of Cusco, calls it Q'entimarka. It must be the original name of Q'entimarka, since Hiram Bingham knew it by this local name. Its boundaries are, to the north, the archaeological site of Qoriwayrachina (agricultural sector); to the south, Aqomoqo and Willkaraqay; to the east, the rural community of Chamana; and to the west, the hill of Casamentuyoc.

The information of the Spanish chroniclers, such as Bernabé Cobo and Santa Cruz Pachacuti, refer that the Urubamba valley, Ollantaytambo and Torontoy, as well as the lands located in the area of Chaullay and Qollpani, belonged to the Inca Pachacuteq, in his process of expansion towards the jungle area, which was used as areas for growing corn and coca leaf. Q'entimarka, would be located within this territory owned by the ninth Inca.

In 1911, Hiram Bingham, on his expedition to find the lost city of Vilcabamba, the last refuge of the Incas, established Salapunku as a base camp for a certain period. He ordered the topographer, Hernan L. Tucker, to cross the Urubamba to explore a small Inca village that could be seen at the other end of the river.

Remaining in the Cusichaca valley for several days, he managed to locate other Inca complexes such as Q'ente, Paucarcancha, Huayllabamba, Incamisana, and Hoccollopampa, saying upon returning from this exploration that the Inca citadel had the name of Patallacta and that it was covered by a lot of vegetation, perhaps that after the destruction and looting in search of gold and silver places, this place had been abandoned by the Inca settlers in their eagerness to escape to the city of Vilcabamba. Hernán Tucker was helped by other people and may have found a lot of archaeological evidence such as ceramics and funerary contexts.

CHAPTER VII: THE TRADITIONAL INCA TRAIL TO MACHU PICCHU (4 DAYS-3 NIGHTS)

The archaeological research work carried out in Llaqtapata was conducted by the archaeologist Ann Kendall in 1978, with her project on the Cusichaca valley, and by the Ministry of Culture of Cusco, under the investigation of archaeologists such as Alfredo Valencia, Luis Tovar, Piedad Champi (2005) or Maritza Rosa Candia (2003).

These archaeologists made findings of fragmented ceramics, from the Formative period, which would belong to the Killki culture, a culture that was established in Cusco, and that had contact with the invading Waris. The Waris influenced their ceramics the type of construction and why not in their religious part. When the Inca lordship was formed in the valley of Cusco as a state or empire from Pachacuteq, in his eagerness to conquer came to these territories.

The village of Q'entimarka, or Llaqtapata, has two periods of occupation: Pre- Inca, and Inca (900 to 1480 AD). The archaeologist Alfredo Valencia, in his article *"History and Evaluation of Archaeological Research in the Historic Sanctuary of Machu Picchu"*, mentions that Patallaqta (or Q'entimarka), would be the largest archaeological complex in the Cusichaca valley, having two main sectors: urban and agricultural:

> *"The urban sector is divided into seven subsectors A, B, C, D, E, F, and G, which contain 23 blocks, 109 enclosures, 38 courtyards, 63 open spaces, 2 monumental staircases, 5 fountains, 3 longitudinal, and 5 transversal passages or streets and 1 plaza.*
>
> *"The agricultural sector contemplates 2 subsectors: High and Low with 15 platforms, with a water channel that crosses the entire trajectory of platform 09, whose main catchment was the waters of the Cusichaca River.*

> *"Due to the characteristics of the complex, it corresponds to a construction of the Inca period, constituting an administrative and control center in the area."*[7]

But it is also important to mention that in every Inca city, whether large, like Machu Picchu, or small, like Q'entimarka, three very important sectors were established: urban, agricultural, and religious.

In Q'entimarka, the urban sector would be located on the slopes of the Casamentuyoc hill, where the largest number of enclosures (dwellings) is located. According to Dr. Alfredo Valencia, there are 109 enclosures dedicated to being inhabited. The question would be: How many people could have lived in the Inca village of Q'entimarka?

In Q'entimarka there are groups of enclosures four in number and other two. They are around a central courtyard. Knowing that the fundamental nucleus of Inca society was the ayllu, which is composed of a large number of people. According to Spanish chronicles, in Inca times, a local family is composed of five or more members (a father, a mother, and three or so children). This is the social class of the people, or hatun runas, and not so in the high or privileged class, were the most important people, chiefs or curacas, had the main wife and several concubines and w i t h t h e m many sons.

Considering that the estimated population of the city of Machu Picchu was no more than seven hundred people, we could very tentatively say that the *llaqta* of Q'entimarka may have had an estimated population of no more than three hundred people.

Here is another question: What kind of people lived in Q'entimarka? And to what social class did these settlers belong?

---

[7] Piedad Champi "Informe Anual de Investigación Arqueológica 2005 del Conjunto Arqueológico de Patallaqta", page 6.

CHAPTER VII: THE TRADITIONAL INCA TRAIL TO MACHU PICCHU (4 DAYS-3 NIGHTS)

Archaeological studies show us that this place was occupied by a pre-Inca culture, the Killkis, and reoccupied in Inca times and based on ethnohistoric data, belonged to the lands of the Inca Pachacuteq.

According to the process of conquest of the Inca State, which began with its greatest territorial expansion during the government of the Inca Pachacuteq, when a village or ethnic group was conquered, the upper-class people were moved to another place, away from their original place, to avoid possible future rebellions. The children of the conquered chiefs or curacas were taken to the capital of Cusco to be indoctrinated in the Inca customs and to be taken as hostages. In case their parents attempted any social movement against the Empire, not only the children were taken hostage but also the idols of their main gods.

We could only say that Q'entimarka was inhabited by very important families from other villages. And the cultivation terraces that are around, as well as the nearby ones like Qoriway-

The village of Qéntimarka, facing east towards the Veronica apu.

rachina and those of the Cusichaca valley, may have been worked by peasants who came from other places under the Inca system of the *Minka*, or work for the Inca government, under the system of labor tax, since in Inca times the monetary system was not known as it is today.

The agricultural sector would be on the hillside, in the lower part of the urban sector towards the Cusichaca River and the cultivation terraces located in the Cusichaca valley, which is still used by local families. They must have cultivated a great variety of corn and potatoes, due to the presence of the Cusichaca River.

We should also mention that for the water supply to the town of Q'entimarka, a water channel was built that was brought from the mountain area of Leonniyoc, passing through the Inca site of Willkaraqay and then descending to the Cusichaca valley and arriving through a small canyon to Q'entimarka.

The religious sector would be located in two places:

1. The area of Pulpituyoc, very close to the Cusichaca River, which is a semicircular construction very similar to the Temple of the Sun in Machu Picchu and Cusco (Q'oricancha), of very simple architecture, having as masonry of large, regular, and small stones, joined with mud mortar. This construction is on top of a rock in situ, which must have been a Huaca.

2. The other ceremonial sector would be located in the site of Willkaraqay, in sector A, according to archaeological evidence. Thus, Q'entimarka and Willkaraqay were a single archaeological complex during the Inca period, as well as a single settlement called Q'entimarka. Having as the main apu to the Veronica mountain, whose orientation is to the east.

# CHAPTER VII: THE TRADITIONAL INCA TRAIL TO MACHU PICCHU (4 DAYS-3 NIGHTS)

Continuing with our hike, after visiting the archaeological site of Willkaraqay and observing Q'entimarka, we will descend through a small ravine, called Leonniyoc and connect with the Cusichaca valley. Towards the right side, about two minutes away, there is a small mountain, with terraces, whose summit must have served as a "control point" or surveillance of the Inca trail, Q'entimarka, and the Cusichaca valley.

From this place, we will walk through the Cusichaca valley, towards the right side. We will see cultivation terraces from the Inca period, which are still used by local families for the cultivation of corn, potatoes, cabbage, carrots, and other agricultural products. To the left side, we will observe rocky mountains, covered by bromeliads, and in the rainy season covered with flowers such as begonias.

About five minutes from the present road, to the left side, you can see evidence of the original Inca trail to Machu Picchu, along with a water channel, which at about ten meters away is covered by vegetation. If one follows the traces of this road, one will arrive at the Tunasmoqo settlement, which is not visited much by tourists. Tunasmoqo can be observed from the lunch spot, called Tarayoc. Most of the groups have lunch in this place because it has hygienic services.

From Tarayoc (from *tara*, a tree of regular size, whose fruits look like red peas or beans, which is used by the local people as medicine for bronchial problems and others) to Hatunchaka (from *hatun*; big and *chaka*; bridge), the landscape is very interesting and beautiful. We observe the presence of small orchids, such as *Wiñaywayana*, or *Epidendrum secundum*, begonias, wild roses, *muña*, or mint, very good for altitude sickness and stomach ache. And fauna such as hummingbirds, sparrows, chihuacos, or hawks. If you are lucky, you will have the opportunity to see sometimes the majestic Andean condor.

In Hatunchaka live local families dedicated to the cultivation of corn and potatoes for family consumption, since many of them have the opportunity to work for the Ministry of Culture, SERNANP, or the Municipality of Machu Picchu Pueblo, as park rangers or workers.

A half-hour hike from Hatunchaka is the village of Huayllabamba, which is the first official campsite. This place is located at an altitude of 3,000 meters/9,840 feet. Nearby, there is another archaeological complex called Patawasi, which is not very visited by hikers. This small complex of Inca culture is highly recommended to be explored in a moment of leisure.

Patawasi

Patawasi is located in the middle of two valleys: Cusichaca and Wayruro, from *wayruro*, a seed of two colors, red and black. For the local people, it means having a lot of luck or fortune. Its UTM coordinates are:

East	North	Altitude (masl and feet)
776551	8532021.6	2,964/9,722

Patawasi was built on an outcrop of metamorphic rock on which ovoid-shaped terraces were built to support it. At the top, five rectangular-shaped enclosures, whose architecture is very simple, made of regular stones joined with mud mortar.

Due to its geographical location, Patawasi must have served as a control point for the Inca trail to Machu Picchu, as well as a control point for the Cusicha valley and the road to the Abra de Pallqay, where small Inca archaeological sites are located, such as Paucarcancha, which can be connected to another very important mountain called the apu Salkantay.

CHAPTER VII: THE TRADITIONAL INCA TRAIL TO MACHU PICCHU (4 DAYS-3 NIGHTS)

The archaeological complex of Patawasi.
It is the control point of the Inca trail to Machu Picchu.

There is another access hike to the citadel of Machu Picchu: it is called "The Salkantay Route". This hike takes five days and four nights and can also be done in four days and three nights. This hike is highly recommended if the tourist does not have the opportunity to hike the trail to Machu Picchu.

Day 2 - The challenge

This day is called the "day of the challenge" because you have to reach the highest point of the hike, the so-called Warmiwañuska Pass, or Dead Woman's Pass. Why this name? Did some local woman or tourist die, and hence the name of this pass? Did the Incas give it this name? What would be the real name of this pass? There are many questions about it, but the answer is given by the place itself. We call it "the pass" because forty-five minutes before reaching the highest point, which is at 4,215 meters/13,825 feet, if you look at the pass, you will see the silhouette of a woman lying down looking up to the sky.

If we want to observe the silhouette of this woman, we have to take, as a reference point, the step itself, which would form the woman's neck. The mountain on the left side would form the face, and on the right side, there is a small mountain that would form the woman's breast. The next mountain would come to be the body, thus giving a profile of a reclining woman. Perhaps this is where the name of this place comes from. Also, when passing 4,000 meters above sea level, the hiker can feel altitude sickness. Perhaps, these two things gave the name to the Paso de la Mujer Muerta (Dead Woman's Pass).

It is important to mention that, in the colonial period, that is, when the Spaniards already dominated the Inca people (in the 16th and 17th centuries), the Spaniards began to write chronicles, visits, documents of a judicial order to name the marking of their new possessions, boundaries or properties. These documents will provide good written information about the names of many places such as towns, mountains, rivers, archaeological or historical sites, and others. Thus, we have within the historical information of the *"Master Plan"* of Machu Picchu, a Spanish document from the mid-seventeenth century found by Dr. Donato Amado Gonzales. This document provides very important information regarding the original names of certain Inca sites and complexes, which are located along the Inca trail to the citadel of Machu Picchu. This information is the *"Documento Silque, 1635-1722"*, Part 14, F.27v., *"Auto de Amparo del reverendo Padre Fray Domingo Cabrera de Lartaun, 29 March 1658"*. This document states:

CHAPTER VII: THE TRADITIONAL INCA TRAIL TO MACHU PICCHU (4 DAYS-3 NIGHTS)

> *"In 1658, after the visit and composition of lands (14) of redress, directed by Fray Domingo Cabrera de Lartaun, the possession, and management of these lands continued with María Cisa, Clara Vispa, Melchora Pata and Lucía Pata, the latter married Don Diego Sanabria Catcorrayo of Cañare ancestry, Principal of the City of San Francisco de Vilcabamba, who achieved the demarcation and delimitation:*
>
> *"(14) The Composition of lands includes, sanitation of the domain through an ancient title invoking the possession of lands, an extension of surrounding lands, acquisition of vacant lands or bacas, without prejudice to the rights of the Indians or third parties"*[8]

This document would allow us to give you the primitive toponymies or the original name of some Inca complexes that are in the stretch between Warmiwañuska and Machu Picchu. In this understanding, the name was given to the Warmiwañuska Pass until 1658 was "Vairurcasa", which could also be "Uaircasa", as it is written in this document.

The name "Uairurcasa", could be understood as Wayrarqasa, which would mean "high point where there is enough wind", which would make more sense, since this point, called Warmiwañuska, is the highest between two valleys, and at certain times there is enough wind.

It is important to mention again the different primitive toponyms of the Inca complexes, places, and rivers such as Runkuraqay, Runkuraqay Pass, Sayacmarka, Intipata, Wiñawayna, Intipunku, Cochapata, and Aobamba River, which are found in this stretch, from the Warmiwañuska sector to the Inca city of Machu Picchu.

---

[8] UPDATE OF THE MACHU PICCHU HISTORIC SANCTUARY MASTER PLAN - DIAGNOSTIC ANNEXES. CUSCO, MARCH 2014. Pages 11-12

> "[...] And from there we go up by a zerro to give to Apu Salcantay that is a Zerronevado that serves as the boundary from where a river called Utimaioba comes to meet the big river of Vilcamayo that serves as boundary and returns bordering with the lands of Nicolas Juarez and the lands of Don Andres Huanca and from there he returns for a knife he will hit the seat of Uairurcasa Puerto where it borders with the lands of Don Nicolas Juares and from there they go down to give to the seat of Rrunco Guasi and from there it goes to give to Yancalla where two lagoons serve as boundary bordering with the lands of Don Balatasar Yepes and from there it goes down by a hill down it goes to give to the seat of Inka Armana that are five pesos of stones that serves as boundary (sic) and borders with the lands/f.32From there it descends by a hill down to give to the seat of Inka Armana that are five pesos of stone that serves as boundary and it borders with the lands of Don Baltasar Yepes to give to Yunca Patamallaucasa Rrucripata that are boundaries and it enters by Arco pongo to Guanapicho where there is half faded (fanegada) of lands and three rooms covered with the straw of which likewise I gave him possession and from here down and go to give to Pumabanca bordering with that of Baltasar Yepes that is the bank of the big river that is called Utimayo and from here go to the lands named Yntiguatanad ondea a n d four rooms covered with straw and I gave him possession of the low lands and house and from there go to give rucmaio pampa that have a bushel of lands that thus I gave him possession...".[9]

When the Spaniards arrived in the Inca territory, they encountered local people who spoke a language different from their native language, Spanish. In Inca times, there were two languages spoken in the Cusco area: Quechua, which was a state

---

9   UPDATE OF THE MESTER PLAN, Ubi Supra.

CHAPTER VII: THE TRADITIONAL INCA TRAIL TO MACHU PICCHU (4 DAYS-3 NIGHTS)

language and was spoken by the common people, and Puquina, which was a language spoken only by the nobility. It must also be understood that other peoples or villages spoke their languages, especially in the jungle area.

The Spaniards, not speaking and understanding the local language of the Inca settlers, had to write or draft their documents (chronicles, visits, judicial writings, and others), according to how they heard the sound of the words by the locals. To understand this, it is better to have an example. Imagine a Peruvian in the country of Holland trying to understand the Dutch language, knowing that the Peruvian is a native speaker of Spanish. The same would be true for a Dutchman wanting to speak the Spanish language. They would not be able to communicate with each other. And even if a person wants to write in his mother tongue a language different from his own.

A porter on the Inca Trail. The local person in charge of loading logistics.

The same must have happened in the 16th and 17th centuries, during the colonial period, when some people may have been able to speak the Quechua language, but could not write it properly, because there was no grammar in this language at that time.

Many hikers, especially those tourists coming from low places above sea level, are afraid that on the way they might have problems with "altitude sickness", which is very common.

The best advice I could give to the trekker is that before doing this trekking he/she should have an acclimatization period in the city of Cusco for 2 or 3 days. This will help a lot. The other thing is the food. When you arrive in the imperial city, the first days you should eat very light food, such as chicken soup, rice, pasta, fruit, and drink plenty of water.

The first camp, called Huayllabamba, is at an altitude of 3,000 meters and the highest point, the Paso de la Mujer Muerta, is at 4,215 meters, as the crow flies. There is a difference of 1,215 meters/3,985 feet in altitude, making 6 kilometers of travel. This entire section is uphill with small slopes and a large number of steps.

The idea of this second day of trekking would be to walk "slowly but surely", or as my American friends say: "take it easy, hold your horses". I prefer to say it locally "take it easy, hold your llamas" since the Inca Trail is an adventure hike and not a marathon or competition.

From the Huayllabamba camp to the pass, as for the local flora, there is a great variety of orchids, begonias, native trees, ferns. The same in terms of fauna, lizards, deer, spectacled bears, foxes, and pumas, all with a variety of landscapes.

From Huayllabamba, an hour and twenty minutes walk uphill, there is a resting place called Ayapata, from *aya*; dead and *pata*, place. Why this name? Because more than twenty years ago, before reaching this place, there is a rock on the left side of the road that

According to Inca Trail regulations, a porter carries between 25 to 26 kilos (logistics and personal equipment).

View of the first step. Note the silhouette of the mountain. It is in the shape of a reclining woman, showing one of her breasts.

has a small hollow, or cave, where there were bone remains a skull and bones. It may have been a pre-Hispanic burial site. And that is where the name comes from. Ayapata is also, today, the first camp for other travel agencies. In this place, there are hygienic services, as well as the opportunity to buy drinks and snacks.

From Ayapata (3,250 meters/10,660 feet) to the next resting place called Llulluchapampa, the hike takes one hour and twenty minutes. But before leaving this place, there is a small gate made of sticks. In this site, more than ten years ago, when clearing vegetation, evidence of the Inca trail to Machu Picchu was found. It was a path made of stones that were possibly more than ten meters long and a meter and a half wide, which today is covered by vegetation. This would show us that there must have been in this place, one of the Inca roads to Machu Picchu.

CHAPTER VII: THE TRADITIONAL INCA TRAIL TO MACHU PICCHU (4 DAYS-3 NIGHTS)

After an hour and twenty minutes of walking, we arrive at the place called Llulluchapampa, from *llullucha* mosses, and *pampa*, place, at the height of 3,800 meters/12,464 feet. In Llulluchapampa there are hygienic services and it is the last place where the hiker will be able to buy drinks and snacks until arriving at the Inca citadel. It is the recommended place to make your last purchases. This section is very interesting. The hiker will cross a mountain forest mixed with local fauna and flora.

From Llulluchapampa to the pass, it takes about an hour and a half. Here, the landscape changes. There is the presence of small bushes, especially when passing 4,000 meters above sea level, that is, at 13,120 feet. We have native trees such as the *queuña*, which was planted by SERNANP to protect the road against future landslides or collapses. And half an hour before arriving at the "pass", one can see how the mountains naturally form the silhouette of the famous reclining woman.

Upon reaching the highest point, the hiker will have the personal satisfaction of having completed his challenge, which is a unique experience, mixed with sweat, physical effort, and emotions.

From the Paso de la Mujer Muerta to the second camp at Pacaymayu, from *pacay*, hidden, and *mayu*, river, at 3,600 meters /11,808 feet, the section of the hike is downhill. The path is paved and in the rainy season it is very slippery, so it is recommended to walk with trekking poles. It is better to walk with four feet than with two. And it is better to walk with four legs. On this descent, at the second camp, you will see in front of you the Inca trail to be followed the next day. In the middle of the trail, you will see a circular Inca construction called Runkuraqay, as well as the second high point called Runkuraqay Pass at 3,950 meters (12,956 feet).

Dead Woman's Pass, or Warmiwañuska, at 4,215 meters/13,825 feet.

The camp of Pacaymayu would mean "hidden river", but according to the Spanish chronicles, Pacaymayu, would refer to the word "Pacay" as the fruit of the *pacae* (guaba, jinicuil), which is a mumosaceous tree of the leguminous family found in South America. It is understood that Pacaymayu would refer to the river where the fruit of the pacae is cultivated.

The new camp is located in the Pacaymayu valley, called the Pacaymayu Alto sector. In the '90s archaeological exploration works were carried out under the direction of the Ministry of Culture Cusco, where archaeologists found a road coming from the Pacaymayu Bajo sector, where the Urubamba valley with its main river is located. This road would show that in Inca times there were several roads that connected to the citadel of Machu Picchu, which connected the valley floor with the archaeological site of Runkuraqay.

CHAPTER VII: THE TRADITIONAL INCA TRAIL TO MACHU PICCHU (4 DAYS-3 NIGHTS)

This Inca trail should be recovered by the Ministry of Culture, or MINCUL, for tourist use and create a new alternative route, connecting it with the Sayacmarka archeological complex.

From Sayacmarca we have another road heading west that descends to the Aobamba valley, where there is another road to go to the site called Hidroeléctrica. Here several archaeological sites of Inca culture exist, such as Intiwatana or Wayratambo, then to travel along one side of the Urubamba River, following the route of the railway line, behind the mountains of Machu Picchu and Huayna Picchu, and finally arriving at the town of Aguas Calientes.

Day 3: The adventure!

The third day is the most interesting before reaching the city of Machu Picchu. The question is why? Because it is the day where the hiker visits, explores, and discovers the magic of this great culture. You will come to understand why in Inca times this trail was used for pilgrimage purposes, as we will discover together.

The advice for day 3 is to wake up very early. Why? Because by waking up and leaving early from Pacaymayu camp, the traveler will have the opportunity to walk - at least the first hour - without many people. He will have the opportunity to feel that he owns this great trail. If the weather is good, he will have the opportunity to see the sunrise, with an incredible view of the Veronica apu. The wonder of this sunrise is the contrast of lights, mountains, and blue sky, especially in the dry season, from May to October.

One hour from the starting point, we arrive at the archaeological site of Runkuraqay. This stretch is paved, but it is not the original Inca trail. From this site, we finally find the original Inca trail. Why? To answer, it would be necessary to understand a little of the history of the Incas, until before the arrival of the Spaniards to the city of Cusco.

In Inca times, the city of Cusco was the capital of the Tawantinsuyo, being rebuilt during the rule of Pachacuteq, in the form of a puma. In this city, there were the most important ceremonial centers of the Empire, such as the Q'oricancha, where the major temples were located, such as those of the Sun, the Moon, the Stars, the Lightning, and the Rainbow, which were decorated with gold and silver plates. Inside these temples, the mummies of the most important Inca rulers were placed, and together with these many offerings. Also, according to the mestizo chronicler Inca Garcilaso de la Vega, outside the Q'oricancha there was an artificial garden with the local flora and fauna, in natural size made of gold and silver.

In addition to Q'oricancha there were other ceremonial sites, such as the palaces of the Incas. All these sites were destroyed and looted by the Spaniards. After the capital, the Spaniards, under the system of extirpations of idolatries made by Polo de Ondegardo, destroyed countless monuments near the city, such as Q'enqo, Tambomachay, Pisac, Urubamba, Ollantaytambo, and other very important religious sites, with the only idea of introducing new culture and new religion to the local Inca settler.

According to mythology, the gods came from the ocean; and the Spaniards arrived by the Peruvian sea. In Inca times, lightning, thunder, and thunderbolt were gods. When the Spaniards used their weapons of war, the Inca settlers must have believed that the conquerors were their gods. Since then, what would a father do if he wanted to protect his family, wife, and children? The answer would be to take the necessary things from the house and start escaping to other places in search of refuge to save his family.

CHAPTER VII: THE TRADITIONAL INCA TRAIL TO MACHU PICCHU (4 DAYS-3 NIGHTS)

It is perhaps after these events that occurred in the city of Cusco and other places. The Incas may have found two places of refuge:

1. It would be the mountains above 4,000 meters/13,120 feet, in places where it is very cold, where the vegetation is of small bushes, with a lot of grass, where the cultivation of some tubers is done, only for family consumption. One of these places could have been the valley of Lares, settlers who maintain the living culture of the Incas, either in their clothing or forms of daily life. The Lares Valley is located three and a half hours by car from the city of Cusco.
2.
3. It would be the jungle (the high jungle, or cloud forest, and the low jungle, or rain forest). The jungle because of the living conditions, climate, poisonous animals, mosquitoes, and other circumstances.

That is why, perhaps after 1537, the Inca citadel of Vilcabamba would be the last refuge of the Incas, being the first ruler of that city, the Inca Manco II, who tried to regain control and government of their ancestors. Manco Inca Yupanqui was a noble Inca, military, political, resistance leader, and first ruler of the independent kingdom of Vilcabamba. He lived in the last years of the Inca Empire and participated in the Inca conquest of the Moxos region. During the civil war between Huáscar and Atahualpa, Manco Inca supported the first one. For what finished the war with the victory of the atahualpista side he had to hide the reprisals of the army of Atahualpa in Cusco. When he received the news of Atahualpa's capture at the hands of the Spaniards, he decided to offer them help, believing that they would free him from the "evil troops of Quito". In exchange for giving them Cusco, the Spaniards named him the Inca emperor, but because of the multiple causes of abuse they committed against him and his people, he decided to escape and rebel.

The war of Manco Inca was the greatest military confrontation of the Conquest of Peru: the Cusco armies cut the roads between Lima and Cusco, besieged both cities, and in 1536 were close to taking Cusco and definitively expelling the Spaniards. However, before the arrival of the Spanish reinforcements of Diego de Almagro and Alonso de Alvarado, Manco took refuge in Vilcabamba because of the excessive time that the war was taking. He led the resistance from his independent kingdom until he was assassinated in 1544, stabbed by a group of seven Almagro Spaniards who betrayed him. Manco II had three successors: Sayri Túpac, Titu Cusi, and Túpac Amaru.

There were thirty-five years of resistance from the Inca people and domination by the Spaniards. Finally, in 1572, the Spaniards arrived in Vilcabamba, destroying the village while killing the local inhabitants, being taken the last Inca of Vilcabamba who was captured and taken to Cusco where he was executed to death by the Spanish invaders.

As the Spanish invaders were looking for Inca ceremonial sites with lots of gold and silver, the Inca settlers created the famous mythical city of El Dorado. According to Inca mythology, El Dorado was an Inca city made of gold, which is why the search for more gold and silver intensified during this period. One of the Spaniards, Francisco de Orellana, organized an expedition to the Amazon in search of this mythical city. The question, does the Inca city of "El Dorado" exist, or is it just a myth? The city of El Dorado "does" exist, it is real. Peruvian explorers or archaeologists know it as the lost city of *Paititi*.

CHAPTER VII: THE TRADITIONAL INCA TRAIL TO MACHU PICCHU (4 DAYS-3 NIGHTS)

I am a member of an NGO in Cusco, the *Inkarri Institute*, constituted of archaeologists, Peruvians, French, Spanish and local people. Our group has located the exact location of this mythical city. We hope, this year, to have the support of the Peruvian government, to be able to make this great archaeological discovery that will change the history of the Incas and modern Peru. But, in the meantime, this city will be hidden in the jungle. I invite you to visit this page: www.granpaititi.com.

Runkuraqay

The Runkuraqay archeological complex is located halfway between the Pacaymayu camp and the second pass (Abra) of Runkuraqay (3,975 meters/13,038 feet). Its UTM coordinates are:

East	North	Altitude (masl and feet)
770780.6	8536292.6	3,768/12,359

This complex was discovered by the American explorer Hiram Bingham in 1915. It was given the name Runkuraqay because it has a circular shape, which in the local language of the Incas, Quechua, Runkuraqay would mean *runku*, deposit, circle, and *raqay*, shed, or house without a roof. This name was given when the explorer asked one of the local people from the peasant community of Huayllabamba who accompanied him.

The name of this place in the documents of Silque, 1635-1722, is Runco Guasi, which can be understood as Runku Wasi, from *runku*, deposit, circle, and *wasi*, house, meaning deposit or house of circular shape.

EXPERT IN ADVENTURE TOURISM

Inca Trail 4D / 3N
Short Inca Trail 2D / 1N
Salkantay Trek 5D / 4N
Lares Trek 4D / 3N
Huchuy Qosqo Trek 3D / 2N
Huchuy Qosqo Trek 2D / 1N
Choquequirau Trek 5D / 4N
Rainbow Mountain
Ausangate Trek 5D / 4N
Very soon! Paititi (El Dorado). The Route the Lost Inca City!

TOURS AROUND OF CUSCO

City Tour
The Incas' Sacred Valley
Machu Picchu by train
Maras and Moray
Pikillacta

EXPERIENCE MORE THAN 20 YEARS IN ADVENTURE TOURISM!

PERU ADVENTURE PEOPLE

www.peruadventurepeople.com
info@peruadventurepeople.com
+51 948001871

FANTASTIC FILMS INTERNATIONAL, LLC AND JUNGLE DOC PRODUCTIONS PRESENT

MACHU PICCHU
THE SECRET CHAMBER
3 x 52 mins

SHOOTING
Alain Bonnet - Thierry Jamin
Edward Valenzuela Gil

SYNOPSIS - TEXTS
Thierry Jamin

VIDEO EDITING
Alain Bonnet

**GRAPHIC DESIGN
SPECIAL EFFECTS - 3D**
Pierre Vaillant - Isham Bandadi
Alain Bonnet

CALIBRATION - CONFORMATION
Laurent Wisshaupt

SOUND
Laurent Duringer

LOGISTIC
José Casafranca Montes

WITH THE VOICES OF
Thierry Jamin
Georges Caudron
Jonnie Hurn

ORIGINAL MUSIC
Michel Wiklacz

FILMMAKING
Alain Bonnet - Thierry Jamin

PRODUCTION
Jungle Doc Productions

ENGLISH VOD

FRENCH VOD

www.fantastic-entertainment.com

For worldwide sales, contact FANTASTIC FILMS INTERNATIONAL at info@ffimail.com

Runkuraqay, or Runku Wasi, is a circular archaeological complex. It has a trapezoidal main entrance and a central circular patio. Around it, there are two elliptical enclosures, inside of which there are small niches. Very close to these two, there are two other enclosures, of small size, and almost quadrangular form, each one with access. The third enclosure of the elliptical form has narrow access but with a view toward the valley of Pacaymayu.

The type of construction at Runkuraqay is of very simple architecture, with blocks of carved stones of rectangular or quadrangular shape and not polished. The stone blocks must have been extracted from the neighboring mountains, which are white granite rocks (plutonic igneous rock composed of 60% quartz, feldspar, and mica), which are joined by a mud mortar.

The archaeological complex of Runkuraqay, also called *Runco Guasi*.

CHAPTER VII: THE TRADITIONAL INCA TRAIL TO MACHU PICCHU (4 DAYS-3 NIGHTS)

For the geographical location where Runkuraqay is located, this archaeological complex dominates the entire Pacaymayu valley, from where you can see the Inca road before and after it. By standing in the middle of the main courtyard or the third

From Runkuraqay, the camp of Pacaymayu and the pass of the Dead Woman can be observed.

enclosure towards the valley, one can see almost to the south very clearly the first Paso de la Mujer Muerta, as well as the road that descends to the second camp. From these details, we could say that Runkuraqay must have been in Inca times a "control or surveillance point" of the Inca trail to the citadel of Machu Picchu.

But very close to Runkuraqay there was a small camp that functioned until before the regulation of the use of the Inca Trail. Near this complex, there was a water spring. This place must have served as a resting place, or tampu, in Inca times, towards Machu Picchu.

From the Runkuraqay complex, we can see the original road, built by the Incas more than five hundred years ago. It was built during the government of Pachacúteq, between 1438 and 1472 approximately. It shows a high degree of constructive engineering, which is still in use today.

After visiting Runkuraqay, there is an hour's walk uphill to the second Runkuraqay Pass, at 3,975 meters/13,038 feet. Twenty minutes before reaching the second pass, to the left side, there is a small lagoon whose name is Cochapata, from *cocha*, lagoon, and *pata*, a place in general. The name of this site in Silque documents is "Yancacalla", today is known as Cochapata.

Like Runkuraqay, until before it was regulated, the Inca trail was a camp, with an excellent view. If the hiker is lucky, he will have the opportunity to see deer, or *tarukas*, wild ducks swimming in the lagoon. Therefore, for the third day, it is advisable to leave very early in the morning to enjoy the landscape, the sunrise, and the observation of the local fauna.

From there you will be able to see towards the front, with an orientation to the cardinal point west, the mountain range of Vilcabamba and in the distance the apu Pumasillo, from *puma*, the feline, and *sillo*, the claw. In this pass, on both sides of the

CHAPTER VII: THE TRADITIONAL INCA TRAIL TO MACHU PICCHU (4 DAYS-3 NIGHTS)

Cochapata lagoon, also called *Yancacalla*.

Inca trail, the traveler can make the rites of offerings to the apus and Pachamama, which in the local tradition, is to place or build columns of stones of different sizes, each one of them being a wish while placing coca leaves or *kintu*. The kintu was the main offering made by pilgrims in Inca times. Today it is still done by local healers or shamans, with the use of "agua de Florida", or water of chance, to purify the place to place the offerings and to purify oneself. Heading east of the pass, also in the distance, you can see the apu Veronica which is very revered in the Sacred Valley of the Incas.

From the second Runkuraqay Pass or Runkuracayqasa, you begin to descend to the next place called Sayacmarka, which takes an hour of walking, of steps, and small slopes made of stones. Half an hour later, on the right side of the road, there is

> The Runkuraqay pass, where the trekker can make some offerings to the apus.

another small dark-colored lagoon called "Yanacocha lagoon", from *yana*, black, and *cocha*, lagoon.

Lugo, five minutes before arriving at Sayacmarka, there is a small viewpoint from where you can see Sayacmarka, as a whole, and in the distance, the mountain range of Vilcabamba, highlighting the apu Pumasillo. From the same viewpoint to the right side, we can see another small archaeological site called Conchamarka and the site of Chakicocha, from *chaki*, or dry, and *cocha*, lagoon. For many trekking groups, this is the lunch spot.

Before starting to climb Sayacmarka, to the left side of the road, there is a small Inca construction of quadrangular shape with small niches inside. Its characteristics show that it must have been a ceremonial source. In Inca times, it must have served as a fountain to perform the purification rite before climbing Sayacmarka.

CHAPTER VII: THE TRADITIONAL INCA TRAIL TO MACHU PICCHU (4 DAYS-3 NIGHTS)

When ascending, there are ninety-seven steps (gradas o peldaños). It is advisable to leave your backpacks on the floor of the road before going up and visiting Sayacmarka.

Sayacmarka

The Sayacmarka archeological site is located on a promontory of a moderate gradient with a northward slope, located in the middle of two streams, Aobamba and Sayacmarka. Its UTM coordinates are:

East	North	Altitude (masl and feet)
769395.1	8536306.4	3,611/11,844

Its limits are, to the north, with the superior canyon of the Aobamba; to the south, with the Runkuraqay pass; to the east,

The archaeological complex of Sayacmarka, also called Inka Armana. This site was a ceremonial center.

with the Inca complex of Qonchamarka; and to the west, with the ravine of the Aobamba valley. The name of this place in the documents of Silque is "Utimayo", having to be the valley of Utimayo as primitive toponymy.

Sayacmarka was discovered by Hiram Bingham in 1915, who named it Cedrobamba. This site, at the time of its discovery, was covered with vegetation, more than 500 years under the jungle literally up to the moment of its discovery.

Twenty-six years later, in 1941, in an expedition led by explorer Paul Fejos, in the "Viking Foundation Expedition", the site of Sayacmarka was rediscovered, carrying out vegetation clearing works. Due to the strategic location and dominance of the valley, he named it Sayacmarka, from *sayac*, to stand, to dominate and *marka*, village, which in the language of the Incas would mean "dominant village" or "inaccessible village". In the documents of Silque the name of this place is "Inka Armana".

After the work done to Sayacmarka by Paul Fejos, in the 1980s and 1990s, under the direction of the Ministry of Culture, important restoration and conservation work has been carried out. Many scholars explain that Sayacmarka could have been in Inca times, a lookout or checkpoint to the city of Machu Picchu. But others say it was a small Inca citadel.

We will allow ourselves to say that Sayacmarka could have been a very important ceremonial center of Inca times. Why? To understand this subject we must understand the religion of the Incas[10].

Similarly, we must understand that the Inca culture in the Peruvian Andes is a "living culture". Why a living culture? Because the Andeans still speak the language of their ancestors, Quechua, or *Runasimi*. Also, they continue to raise llamas and alpacas in their mountains. They continue to grow corn and pota-

---

[10] See chapter IV

CHAPTER VII: THE TRADITIONAL INCA TRAIL TO MACHU PICCHU (4 DAYS-3 NIGHTS)

toes as their main crops; they continue to chew coca leaves and venerate the Apus and Pachamama.

If we ask the local people: Do you still worship the Sun, the Moon, the Stars, the Rainbow? The answer will be simple: the sun is the sun, the moon is the moon. But if we ask the same people, today, if they worship or venerate their apus, the answer will be a simple yes, why? Because the apus provide the element of water. In our local concept, it is very easy to understand if one is a farmer, who grows corn, potatoes, or any product. You need the element of water. The same if you are a shepherd, you need better pastures for your animals. It is a simple rule: "if there is no water, there is no life".

Now, it is understood when the Inca people worshiped the mountains with snow, such as the Ausangate apu. This glacier can be observed when hiking on the trekking of the "Montaña de Colores" (Colored Mountain). Because the water element constantly descends from the snow-capped mountains. The question would be then: Why did the Incas worship the mountains, knowing that in the Andes there are not hundreds, but thousands of mountains? Because, in some mountains, not in all, there are waterfalls, springs, lakes, lagoons, large or small rivers. So we come to the same conclusion: it is the element of water. Without water, there is no life.

This veneration to the apus was perhaps a tradition that was practiced since pre- Inca, Inca, colonial times and continues today in the inhabitant especially in the city of Cusco. Like the Pachamama, offerings are made to them, being coca, mullu, corn, llama, or alpaca fetus or bait as the most appreciated offerings.

In Sayacmarca, there are several important constructions. When climbing the steps, at the end towards the left side there is an almost rectangular platform that must have been in Inca times an *usnhu*, or main altar. On this altar, the Incas must have performed their ceremonies and offerings to the apu Pumasillo. If we use a compass, we will see that the entire archaeological complex is oriented toward the west in the direction of the apu Pumasillo.

Another important enclosure that is next to this altar, is a semicircular construction that some scholars give the term of accommodation, or kallanka. This enclosure is very important especially if the hiker pays attention: between May and July, that is, before and after the winter solstice. In the Peruvian Andes it is every June 21st, is located in the southern hemisphere, being different from the northern hemisphere, where the summer solstice is celebrated.

During the winter solstice, at sunrise, the sun rises from the east side, where the Veronica apu is located. When it reaches the top of this mountain, it will illuminate, at first, the Runkuraqay Pass, and then illuminate the Pumasillo apu, whose orientation is to the west. After that, as the sun descends, it will illuminate only

Apu Pumasillo. In the winter solstice, the sun with the mountains will form in the shadow the silhouette of a puma

CHAPTER VII: THE TRADITIONAL INCA TRAIL TO MACHU PICCHU (4 DAYS-3 NIGHTS)

Sayacmarka. It is like this action when a person takes a powerful flashlight in the dark and points to a single specific place: you can only see the illuminated point within a circle and outside this, everything is dark.

It is the same action that takes place in Sayacmarka: the sun first illuminates this semicircular construction and then advances toward the central part, where there is a Huaca; and after a few minutes, the sun illuminates the entire site. This phenomenon can be observed by hikers who sleep the second day at the Chakicocha camp.

On your way to Phuyupatamarka Pass, approximately twenty-five minutes from Chakicocha, you will see that on the right side of Sayacmarka there is a small chain of mountains, and very close to them there is a waterfall. When the sun shines on this small mountain, a shadow can be seen above it, slowly drawing the image or silhouette of a puma's head. Perhaps, for this reason, the apu Pumasillo has taken this name.

In Sayacmarka, in the central part, there is also a huaca that presents, in one of the sides, the image of an Inca priest, in jumping or moving position, holding in both hands some objects, perhaps a *kero*, or ceremonial vessel, and a *maraka*, or another similar object, giving Sayacmarka its religious aspect.

The Sayacmarka Huaca, located in the central part of the ceremonial center.

Throughout this archaeological site, there are eighteen enclosures, which must have served as homes for the upper and priestly class who made this religious pilgrimage to the city of Machu Picchu.

From Sayacmarka we follow a path that goes in the direction of the Aobamba valley, passing by the waterfall sector, which is still hidden by vegetation. This route was located in the '90s, by archaeologists of the Ministry of Culture of Cusco.

Because of the type of vegetation, Sayacmarka must have been accessing the high jungle, or cloud forest. After exploring the site, after a five-minute walk, we arrived at the archaeological site of Qonchamarka.

Qonchamarka

This archaeological site of Qonchamarka, from *qoncha*, seashell, spondylus, in Quechua it is called mullu, and *marka*, village, is located on the right bank of the stream that flows down from the Yanacocha lagoon and the Inca trail, in the direction of Chakicocha. Its UTM coordinates are as follows:

East	North	Altitude (masl and feet)
769215.9	8536461.9	3,567/11,700

Qonchamarka has as base and construction support, of two terraces of semicircular form in form of "U", that looks like a marine shell, or spondylus, for which it would have the name of the place. In the upper part, there are three rectangular enclosures built with unpolished carved stone blocks, of regular size, joined with mud mortar, the same ones that must have had roofs, made of straw, or ichu, in the Inca period. Towards the left side of the

CHAPTER VII: THE TRADITIONAL INCA TRAIL TO MACHU PICCHU (4 DAYS-3 NIGHTS)

road, in the vegetation, some rectangular constructions could have been used as dwellings.

Because of its location near Sayacmarka, Qonchamarka must have served as a small tampu, or resting place, or a "checkpoint" on the Inca trail. Near this site, there is a small river that comes from the upper part of the Yanacocha lagoon.

From Qonchamarka, the trail is more moderate with small ascents and descents. You can observe a great variety of local flora of the high jungle ecosystem such as mosses, ferns, small trees, bromeliads, orchids, begonias.

On the left side, you have incredible views of the Aobamba valley, or Utimayo, and the Vilcabamba mountain range. Then, after a half-hour walk, you arrive at the place called Chakicocha, from *chaki*, dry, and *cocha*, lagoon. This is the lunch spot for most of the groups. In this place, you will find hygienic services.

The archaeological complex of Qonchamarka. A small tampu.

From Chakicocha, the Inca complex of Sayacmarka can still be seen in the distance. Because of the geographical location of this archaeological complex, located on top of a small promontory, the hiker will understand why some scholars explain that Sayacmarka was a fortress or a control point of the Inca trail.

Passing Chakicocha there is a small stream and a modern bridge built with sticks of trees. In this place, the road is paved and there is a small flat section, very interesting. Towards the end, before ascending to the left side, there is another original road that is also paved, which is not very noticeable because it is covered with vegetation. This would be another road that leads to the city of Machu Picchu.

The altar, from where the apu Salkantay is observed
It is located five minutes before reaching the Inca tunnel.

CHAPTER VII: THE TRADITIONAL INCA TRAIL TO MACHU PICCHU (4 DAYS-3 NIGHTS)

The apu Salkantay, the highest mountain in the Vilcabamba range.

Forty minutes before reaching the Inca tunnel we find another medium-sized usnhu, from where we can observe the most important apu of the Vilcabamba mountain range: the Salkantay, from *salka*, wild, uncivilized, and *tay*: mountain. By using a compass again we will see how this mountain is oriented towards the south, while the Pumasillo apu is oriented towards the west; and a third apu, the Phuyupatamarka Pass, with direction towards the north.

After a ten minute walk, we will cross the famous Inca tunnel. This tunnel, about twenty-five years ago, was smaller; and before going through it we had to climb some small steps. The Ministry of Culture reconstructed this section of the road and enlarged the tunnel.

Half an hour into the journey, we will arrive at a "false pass", from where the hiker will be able to observe the Salkantay, Pumasillo, and Veronica apus. On both sides of the pass, to the left side of the road, we can see the Aobamba valley or Utimayo, and to the right side, the Urubamba valley.

Then, about twenty or twenty-five minutes before reaching the third Phuyupatarmarka Pass, on the right side of the road, at ground level, there is a small altar that has been carved into the rock, giving it the shape of three levels, whose main corner has a

The Inca tunnel. The rock was carved for the construction of the road

CHAPTER VII: THE TRADITIONAL INCA TRAIL TO MACHU PICCHU (4 DAYS-3 NIGHTS)

cardinal orientation to the west and the apu Pumasillo, which can be verified by using a compass.

Arriving at the third pass, Phuyupatamarka, at 3,600 meters/11,808 feet, you can see the Veronica and Salkantay apus, and in the distance the Machu Picchu mountain. Behind this is the famous Inca citadel, and on the left side, you have the archaeological site of Intipata, from *inti* sol, and *pata*, place or village. You can also see the archaeological site of Phuyupatamarka.

Five minutes from the Phuyupatamarka Pass, walking downhill is the Inca complex of Phuyupatamarka.

Phuyupatamarka

The archaeological site of Phuyupatamarka is located on the slope of a mountain with a marked gradient, which is connected by the Inca trail, as it crosses the Inca complex. Phuyupatamarca is within the Vilcabamba mountain range and its UTM coordinates are:

East	North	Altitude (masl and feet)
767491	8538723.5	3,604/11,821

This site was discovered in 1915 by Hiram Bingham, who named it Qoriwayrachina, from *qori*, gold, and *wayrachina*, "the place where the wind blows" or "the place where the wind runs".

Like Sayacmarka, Phuyupatamarka was covered with vegetation at the time of its discovery, more than five hundred years under the jungle. In 1941, explorer Paul Fejos rediscovered this site, changing it to the current name of Phuyupatamarka, from *phuyu*, clouds, and *marka*, a town, which means "a town above the clouds", since this Inca complex rises in the middle of a pit,

The archaeological complex of Phuyupatamarka, also called *Mallaucasa*.

where the clouds remain below it, without being altered by the wind, thus giving the current name to the archaeological complex.

In the documents of Silque the name of this place is "Mallaucasa", and it could be Mallauqasa.

To better understand what Phuyupatamarka, or Mallauqasa, was in Inca times, we will have to divide it into several sectors:

1. Before entering Phuyupatamarka, to the left side of the road, we find a water fountain, which was built with stone masonry, in white granite, slightly polished. To the interior of this one, it has several small niches of trapezoidal form, in which small offerings should have been placed. In this place, there is a water spring that runs along one side of the complex. This fountain must have been used for water worship ceremonies. Very close to this are five other

CHAPTER VII: THE TRADITIONAL INCA TRAIL TO MACHU PICCHU (4 DAYS-3 NIGHTS)

fountains, in a straight line, where the water flows, which could have been used for "purification" ceremonies.
2. The platform at the top, semicircular in shape, has a very different architecture from the other constructions. It is made of stone masonry, more elaborate, and is joined one to the other without the use of any mud mortar, unlike the others.

This platform was in the process of construction and was not finished. Here would be three questions: Would this construction be dedicated to build a temple? And because before accessing it, there is evidence of double jamb access, a sign that a ceremonial or religious precinct was being built? The third question would be: Was a large usnhu being built? This is oriented to the north, towards the Machu Picchu mountain, and can be seen very clearly. Behind the mountain is the famous Inca citadel.

3. There are several levels of terraces, or platforms, that would serve to protect and support the entire archaeological complex, the same that could have served for the cultivation of some agricultural products.
4. In front of the platform, we observe two open semicircular enclosures that could have served as resting places. In each of them, there is a rectangular enclosure (living places), which could have been occupied by the people in charge of this Inca site (priests), and in the lower part, there are several quadrangular enclosures that could have been used as qollqas, or deposits.
5. On leaving this complex, a minute away, to the left side of the Inca trail, there are two caverns that may have been used as places where the stone carvers hid during the

rainy season or to protect themselves from the sun. These are covered by vegetation today.

Phuyupatamarka, with all these sectors as a whole, would be a very important ceremonial or religious center on the way to the city of Machu Picchu, a place of pilgrimage.

From the Phuyupatamarka complex, very close to the third pass, towards the left side of the road, we find a mountain that, in its upper part or summit, has a circular platform built with masonry of worked stones, joined one to the other without mud mortar.

This platform must have been another altar, or usnhu, since there is a small carved rock that is oriented towards the apu Salkantay. This rock has the shape or silhouette of the apu Salkantay, the largest apu in the Vilcabamba mountain range. Likewise, from this place you can see very clearly all the mountains that surround the city of Machu Picchu: to the north, the Machu Picchu mountain, at 3,100 meters/10,168 feet; to the south, the apu Salkantay, at 6,270 meters/20,566 feet; to the east, the apu Veronica, at 5,750 meters/18,860 feet; and to the west, the apu Pumasillo at 6,000 meters/19,680 feet. From this place, there is a predominant view of the Urubamba and Aobamba valleys. This usnhu must have served as a place for religious ceremonies and also, due to its strategic location, as a place to observe the Milky Way, the stars, and constellations, especially on the winter solstice, June 21st, where the constellation of the Southern Cross stands out.

The sad thing about this platform is that it has been huaqueada, or destroyed by people who are only looking for treasures and have no respect for the culture. This is because in this place, until today, there is evidence of several holes. Who made them? We

CHAPTER VII: THE TRADITIONAL INCA TRAIL TO MACHU PICCHU (4 DAYS-3 NIGHTS)

will leave that answer to the conscience of those who are in charge of the Inca Trail and the archaeological site.

If we join these two places, the mountain with the platform and the Inca complex, Phuyupatamarka, would have served as a very important ceremonial or religious center on the way to the citadel of Machu Picchu, as well as an astronomical observation center.

From Phuyupatamarka, the Inca trail is only downhill, a mixture of steps and slopes, but with a cobblestone road, a little slippery in the rainy season. The use of trekking poles is highly recommended.

Twenty-five minutes downhill, to the left side of the road, there is a large cave in which the Incas took advantage of the natural

View of Machu Picchu from Phuyupatamarka.

fault in the rock to use it as a resting place. Towards the right side of the cave, there is an Inca wall.

After 45 minutes of walking, we arrive to find two quadrangular enclosures that must have been small tampus (resting places) and an open quadrangular platform, from where you can see the Machu Picchu mountain and the Inca complex of Intipata and the Urubamba Mountain Range.

After this Inca site, the Inca trail has the form of a spiral with a large number of steps and then passes through another small tunnel. From this tunnel, the road is smoother. At about forty-five minutes you have an electric tower, where there is a wooden sign where the Inca Trail divides.

If you turn right, the trail is short. After a forty-minute walk (dirt road), you will arrive at the Wiñaywayna camp. But if you take the road to the left (recommended road), in fifteen minutes you will arrive at the Inca complex of Intipata. From this site to the Wiñaywayana camp the hike takes about forty-five minutes.

Intipata

This archaeological site is located on the left bank of the Urubamba River, in the upper part of the Urubamba Valley, in the high jungle ecological floor, very close to the Machu Picchu mountain. Its UTM coordinates are:

East	North	Altitude (masl and feet)
766489.1	8541008.7	2,750/9,020

Intipata was also discovered by Hiram Bingham in 1915 who gave it the name of Intipata. It was covered by vegetation. Its original name, in Inca times, could have been "Yunkapata", from *yunka*, or hot lands, burning lands, and *pata*, a village located in the upper part, which would make more sense.

CHAPTER VII: THE TRADITIONAL INCA TRAIL TO MACHU PICCHU (4 DAYS-3 NIGHTS)

In 1940, Paul Fejos, between November and December, carried out archaeological work, finding one hundred and fifteen tombs very close to Intipata, three of which were disturbed. These discoveries added to the findings made by Hiram Bingham in the northern area of the mountain of Machu Picchu and around the Inca citadel provide the information that Machu Picchu was populated by a large number of people.

In 1969, 1995, 1997 and 1999, archaeologists Manuel Chávez Ballón, Octavio Fernández, Rene Pilco and Sabino Quispe found archaeological evidence such as agricultural tools: *q'asunas*, star-shaped *kupanas*, hammers, knives, and ceramic fragments for domestic use, such as pots and plates. These pieces of evidence demonstrate an occupation of farming families.

To understand Intipata or Yunkapata, we must divide it into several sectors:

The archaeological complex of Intipata, also called *Yunkapata*. Agricultural center.

1. In the upper part, we find two rows of enclosures, each of them with eight enclosures, which must have served as dwellings for the peasants who came in times of paying the labor tax, to perform agricultural work (planting and harvesting). The permanence of these peasants was for a short period in which they cooked.
2. The largest number of constructions at Intipata are terraces for agricultural use. It is important to know that Intipata is at 2,750 meters/9,020 feet. Because of its location in the high jungle, it could be assumed that in these agricultural terraces, *cassava, sweet potato,* corn, *aguaymanto, rocotos* and mainly coca leaf could have been cultivated.
3. In the middle part of the agricultural terraces sector, we found three rectangular-shaped enclosures, which may have served as dwellings for the families who were in charge of the site.
4. The qollqas sector is located on the left side of the Inca trail, at the beginning of Intipata. In this place, there is a wooden sign that says "Intipata". At present this place is covered with vegetation. In these qollqas, the crops could have been stored to supply the city of Machu Picchu with some agricultural products.
5. In the lower part, already to leave Intipata, there is an open rectangular enclosure on a platform. It could have been an altar, which must have been used to perform certain religious ceremonies. Hidden in the vegetation, still exist many Inca constructions that are waiting to be cleaned and restored for their conservation.

As a whole, the interesting thing about Intipata is that it is oriented to the east towards the sunrise, clearly observing the apu Veronica or Wakay Willka.

CHAPTER VII: THE TRADITIONAL INCA TRAIL TO MACHU PICCHU (4 DAYS-3 NIGHTS)

In Intipata, for the agricultural terraces and dwellings, the type of architecture is simple, made of carved stones, not polished, joined with mud mortar. The stone masonry is of white granite. They must have been extracted from the neighboring mountains.

Intipata was an agricultural complex that must have been used once a year, that is, only during the rainy season, when the peasants used the enclosures located in the upper part as a place to live. But it also has a ceremonial place, or usnhu, to perform perhaps the rites of planting and harvesting, which were very common in Inca times.

From Intipata to Wiñaywayna, the last camp, it is a thirty-minute walk. Most trekkers arrive at this camp very late. Therefore the advice to leave the second camp (Pacaymayu), very early to have the opportunity to visit the complex of Wiñaywayna (highly

View of the Urubamba valley from Intipata.

recommended to be visited). This Inca complex is ten minutes away from the camp.

Wiñaywayna

The archaeological site of Wiñaywayna is located on the left bank of the Urubamba River, in the middle part of the mountain between the river and the Inca complex of Intipata, as well as on the left side of the stream that flows down from Phuyupatamarka. It is on the ecological floor of a high jungle, or cloud forest. Wiñaywayna is built on a rocky promontory on the mountainside, with very rugged topography. Its UTM coordinates are:

East	North	Altitude (masl and feet)
767023.5	8540204	2,655/8,708

In 1941, thirty years after the discovery of Machu Picchu, Wiñaywayna was discovered by chance by explorer Paul Fejos, who was in charge of the "Expedition Viking Fund" of New York.

The following year, the Peruvian archaeologist Julio Cesar Tello rediscovered it still hidden in the vegetation. It was given the name Wiñaywayna because in this area there is a variety of orchids. From *wiñay*, to grow, forever, and from *wayna*, young; which would mean "forever young". This orchid specifically blooms twice a year, in the rainy season and in the dry season. However, the name of this place in Silque documents is "Rrucripata".

From the work done by archaeologist J.C. Tello, who must have carried out vegetation clearing work, he must have found in this complex, at floor level, evidence of archaeological material such as pottery (pots, plates, spinning wheels), and other archaeological materials, such as metal objects.

CHAPTER VII: THE TRADITIONAL INCA TRAIL TO MACHU PICCHU (4 DAYS-3 NIGHTS)

After Dr. Tello's archaeological work, local archaeologists from the Ministry of Culture carried out excavation work at different sites. On the occasion of these investigations, they discovered fragments of Inca-style ceramics as well as *t'ipanas*, or metal pins and clay spinning wheels. These elements provide evidence that Wiñawayna could have been inhabited by a group of craftswomen dedicated to the manufacture of textiles or clothing. Because there are a large number of *masmas*, in the lower part of the Inca complex, open rectangular enclosures with three walls and a thatched roof, to protect themselves from the rain or the sun.

Based on this evidence, archaeologists explain that Wiñaywayna could have been a small Inca village occupied by the mitmas, or people sent by the Inca State to populate the conquered territories and teach the inhabitants the customs of the Sons

The archaeological complex of Wiñaywayna, also called *Rrucripata*.

of the Sun. At the top, there is a tower, or semicircular construction, which served as a checkpoint.

To better understand what Wiñaywayna, or Rrucripata, may have been in Inca times, it should be divided into several sectors:

1. The upper sector, where the so-called "tower" is located. This construction could have been dedicated to the worship of the god K'uychi, or rainbow. Why the rainbow? Because Wiñaywayna is located in the high jungle. In this place, there is the presence of water, in its liquid (rain) and gaseous (clouds or fog) states, knowing that in the Peruvian Andes, we have two seasons: rainy season and dry season. Even in this sector in the dry season, it's raining. In the high jungle, the sun is quite strong or bright. When this natural phenomenon happens – very sunny - mixed with the presence of clouds or rains, a natural phenomenon of a prism is produced, which will give rise to the creation, facing east, towards the Urubamba valley, of a great rainbow. Sometimes you can see two rainbows: in the belief of the people of the Andes, male and female. So this semicircular construction has been dedicated to the veneration of the god Kuychi. To this is added the double jamb entrance doorway to this enclosure, giving importance to this construction.
2. In the middle part of the complex, there are several quadrangular water fountains, with small niches inside where offerings could have been placed. There are also water channels, carved in the upper part, through which water flows all year round. These fountains, like the city of Machu Picchu, may have had two uses: one to provide water to the site and two, to perform purification rites. We go for the second explanation, that they would have served to perform purification rites, before reaching Machu Picchu.

CHAPTER VII: THE TRADITIONAL INCA TRAIL TO MACHU PICCHU (4 DAYS-3 NIGHTS)

3. The cultivation terraces, which cover a large area in this complex. Because of the altitude where Wiñaywayna is located, in the high jungle, at 2,700 meters/8,856 feet, several agricultural products such as yucca, sweet potato, corn, chili, and especially coca leaf, must have been cultivated. It was probably taken from here to the Sacred Valley of the Incas, to the city of Cusco, and other places, where it was not possible to cultivate these products. All this agricultural sector is oriented towards the east (sunrise), overlooking the Urubamba valley and the apu Veronica.
4. The urban sector, the enclosures, and the masmas, or shelters, were occupied as dwellings. From the number of enclosures, we can indicate that it did not have a large number of people or families. These people would be dedicated to the

Wiñaywayna, was possible "the last spiritual resting place" before reaching the Inca citadel of Machu Picchu.

task of making textiles or would be in charge of the care and protection of this place.
5. There are still many other places (enclosures and terraces), which are covered with vegetation, waiting to be discovered, to have a better understanding of what Wiñaywayna could have been in Inca times.

Wiñaywayna, due to its characteristics as a whole, must have been "the last stop for spiritual rest" before reaching the city of Machu Picchu, a two-hour walk away. The whole complex is oriented towards the east, that is, towards the Urubamba valley and the apu Veronica.

It is in Wiñaywayna where you have the largest number of ceremonial fountains, before reaching Machu Picchu. If we make a difference with the rest of the archaeological complexes that are along the Inca Trail, it is the most beautiful complex in terms of its construction design and type of architecture.

Day 4 - Machu Picchu - We did it!

The last day of the trek is a bit stressful, why? Because the trekkers have to get up very early. Many groups get up between 3 and 3:30 a.m. Why so early? Because the porters have to take the train back to the village of Ollantaytambo (5:30 am).

For this, the most advisable thing to do on the last night is to go to bed very early and have your backpack ready to take with you to Machu Picchu (last day).

Some travel agencies offer breakfast service at the campsite and others offer a small snack, consisting of a cheese sandwich, juice, fruit, and a coffee or chocolate. It would be advisable for the hiker to take some good snacks for the last day. The other option would be, before visiting Machu Picchu, to enjoy a hot drink or sandwiches.

CHAPTER VII: THE TRADITIONAL INCA TRAIL TO MACHU PICCHU (4 DAYS-3 NIGHTS)

Near the entrance control in the sacred city, there is a small cafeteria that offers many products, where the hiker should also make use of the toilets, as in Machu Picchu, it will not be possible.

The hiker will be in line for more than an hour since the Wiñaywayna checkpoint opens at 5.30 am. Here you have to show your passport (a very important document).

The walk from Wiñaywayna to Inti Punku takes 1 hour. In some sectors, it is very narrow. It is recommended to walk very slowly. It is easier to understand it this way: "Machu Picchu does not move, it was, is, and will be forever in the same place", "hold your llamas".

Twenty minutes before arriving at Inti Punku, you have the famous "gringo killer". The Inca trail is very steep and has many steps. At the end of this, there is a small construction that in Inca times must have served the function of control and surveillance. From this point to Inti Punku it is a twelve-minute walk. Arriving at the Puerta del Sol, the feeling is great, full of emotions, and fulfilled dreams.

Before reaching Inti Punku, the Inca trail is very steep, which is why this segment is known as the "gringo killer".

Inti Punku, the Sun gate

Inti Punku is a small Inca archaeological site, close to the city of Machu Picchu, one kilometer away. Its UTM coordinates are:

East	North	Altitude (masl and feet)
767320.3	8542814.6	2,650/8,692

The name of this place in the Silque documents is "Arcopongo", and it seems to be a word composed of two languages: Spanish and Quechua (or Quechuan), where "arco" would mean, an arch, geometric shape, and "pongo", could be understood as punku, which means door in the Quechua language.

From Inti Punku, or Arcopongo, you can see in the distance the city of Machu Picchu, the Urubamba valley and the mountain of Huayna Picchu, huayna, or young, and Picchu, mountain.

Inti Punku, the Gate of the Sun, also called *Arcopongo*.

CHAPTER VII: THE TRADITIONAL INCA TRAIL TO MACHU PICCHU (4 DAYS-3 NIGHTS)

Inti Punku, because of its location, on a high point between the Inca Trail and the citadel, must have served as access control. Likewise, it must have served as an observation point for the summer solstice, on December 22nd.

The type of architecture is simple: white granite stone masonry joined with mud mortar, the rectangular enclosure with four access openings, front and back, and inside trapezoidal niches. In the summer solstice, if you are very lucky, that is, good weather, with a sunny day without clouds, you can see how the sun crosses the Inti Punku through these four access openings, illuminating the Intipunku, and then the city of Machu Picchu. Towards the citadel, you can see that Inti Punku was built on a base of containment platforms taking advantage of the geomorphology of the mountain.

The Inca altar, on the descent to Machu Picchu, where pilgrims possibly placed offerings before reaching the sacred city.

THE INCA TRAIL TO MACHU PICCHU

As we descend to Machu Picchu, the hiker can take good pictures. Halfway between Inti Punku and Machu Picchu, on the right side of the road, we find an altar. It is perhaps the largest carved in the rock, where those who came to Machu Picchu to celebrate the most important festivities, may have placed their offerings. This ceremony is still done today. Behind this formation, we find rectangular constructions that must have served as a control point and access to Machu Picchu.

From this usnhu, about twenty-five minutes downhill, the hiker will reach Machu Picchu where he will observe a large number of tourists taking the classic photos: Machu Picchu city and behind it, the mountain of Huayna Picchu. Once you have taken your photos, we recommend you to go down to the last checkpoint to visit the citadel.

Classic photo of Machu Picchu, at the end of this great adventure.

CHAPTER VII: THE TRADITIONAL INCA TRAIL TO MACHU PICCHU (4 DAYS-3 NIGHTS)

Recommendation before visiting the Inca citadel of Machu Picchu:

1. Use the hygienic services, since during the visit to the city you will not be able to count on "bathrooms".
2. If the hiker has a backpack of more than twenty-five liters, it will have to be stored in the checkroom, since it is not allowed to carry it inside the Inca city. It is only allowed to carry small backpacks of a maximum of twenty liters.
3. For the visit to Machu Picchu, bring your original passport and show your student card, if you have one, at the entrance of the Inca Trail.
4. Carry in your backpack bottles (glass or metal) of water, "snacks", such as cookies, energy bars, such as chocolates or snickers. Keeping the garbage in your backpack or pocket.
5. Dress in the clothes that the hiker feels most comfortable since Machu Picchu is located in the high jungle and has two seasons (rainy and dry), sunglasses, caps, hats, rain ponchos, if necessary, sunscreen, mosquito repellent.

Prepared and ready for the visit. We start with the visit to Machu Picchu.

Note: The Ministry of Culture of Cusco is the government entity in charge of regulating the visit of the Inca city, having three routes: long, medium, and short. This regulation came into operation in 2019. For better enjoyment of this great experience, after having walked for four days, we will take the first option: the long tour.

THE INCA TRAIL TO MACHU PICCHU

SHORT INCA T
2 D

Cusco city

Highway

Urubamba

Ollantaytambo

Urubamba River

km. 104

2,6

Cat

Railway Line

Legend:
- - - - - Inca Trail
🛕 Inca Complex
⊙ Town
━━━ River
◊ Lagoon
┼┼┼┼┼┼┼ Railway Line
🏛 Waterfall

DISEÑO REALIZADO POR
CHARLY CÁRDENAS LÓPEZ
DISEÑADOR GRÁFICO
E-MAIL REYFENIX@HOTMAIL.COM

TO MACHU PICCHU
/ 1 NIGHT

yna
ata)
,708 feet

Inti Punku
(Arcopongo)
2,650 mts / 8,692 feet

9 mts
14 feet
amba

Choquesuysuy
2,163 mts
7,095 feet

Bus route

Aguas Calientes Pueblo

Hidroelectrica

THE INCA TRAIL TO MACHU PICCHU

CHAPTER VIII
THE SHORT INCA TRAIL TO MACHU PICCHU (2 DAYS AND 1 NIGHT)

Another trek to Machu Picchu is the Inca Trail of 2 days and 1 night. This formula is recommended for trekkers who do not have enough time to do the traditional circuit of four days and three nights. This option allows the trekker to make a reservation without many months in advance since in most cases there are plenty of spaces available (200 spaces each day).

Day 1 - The adventure!

On the first day, we leave Cusco very early in the morning by car. The trip takes about two hours, so the hiker has to get up very early (3:00 or 3:30 am). Get ready and wait for the transportation.

You should leave the city no later than 4:00 am. Arriving at the town of Ollantaytambo (train station), you have the option to enjoy a light breakfast. The most advisable option to enjoy the trip is to take the train at 6:10 am. Why? Because it is the first tourist train that leaves for Machu Picchu. The tourist will have

THE INCA TRAIL TO MACHU PICCHU

all the time in the world to enjoy this great adventure, plus there will not be many hikers on the Inca Trail.

The train ride from Ollantaytambo to kilometer 104, our starting point, takes approximately one hour and fifteen minutes. The train ride is extraordinary for many reasons: the variety of landscapes, the ecosystems, the view of the Urubamba River, etc. On the way, you will be able to see several archaeological complexes of Inca culture, which are located on both banks of the Urubamba River, such as Salapunku, Qhanabamba, Q'entimarka, Qoriwayrachina. The journey by train is very interesting.

When you reach km 104, before reaching the Inca Trail checkpoint, you will cross a bridge where you will have an incredible view of the Urubamba River. At the checkpoint, permits and passports must be presented. In this place, the hiker has the option to buy some drinks, snacks and use the restroom. Two minutes' walk away is the first Inca complex called Chachabamba.

Chachabamba

The archaeological site of Chachabamba is located on the left side of the Urubamba River, at km 104, on the train route from Cusco to Machu Picchu. Chachabamba is located in the high jungle and its UTM coordinates are:

East	North	Altitude (masl and feet)
769862.6	8540913.6	2,169/7,114

In 1915, one of the members of the Yale expedition led by Hiram Bingham, such as the assistant topographer Clarence Maynard, found this very interesting Inca complex. It is located only two kilometers from Choquesuysuy, and it must have been found by the same person since there is an Inca road that connects both sites.

CHAPTER VIII THE SHORT INCA TRAIL TO MACHU PICCHU (2 DAYS-1 NIGHT)

In 1944, Paul Fejos carried out research work. He must have found all this complex covered with vegetation. He also had to carry out cleaning works and find archaeological evidence, such as ceramics and lithic elements: hammers and metals such as knives.

After the work carried out by Paul Fejos, the Ministry of Culture of Cusco also carried out several excavation and restoration works for the preservation of this site, finding fragments of Inca-style ceramics, metal objects, and stone hammers.

Chachabamba is made up of several structures: there are fourteen rectangular enclosures. Some are built with three walls and in the middle part, there is a pillar to support the thatched roofs that must have been used to house the people who were on their way to the city of Machu Picchu.

The archaeological complex of Chachabamba. Main altar.

In the central part, there is a large altar carved in rock, which must have been used for ceremonies or human or animal sacrifices. It is necessary to explain that, in Inca times, it was very common to make animal sacrifices, especially a black llama. For the Inca religion, the llama was considered a sacred and important animal for three reasons: food, transportation and to provide wool for the manufacture of clothing. Moreover, the color black in the Inca religion signifies purity, the opposite of the Catholic or other religions.

In the time of the Tawantinsuyo, in very extreme cases such as natural catastrophes, landslides, floods, too much rain, or natural phenomena such as El Niño or La Niña, or when a new ruler took office, the Incas performed a ceremony called Cápacocha. On that occasion, "if" human sacrifices were performed. A clear example of this is the great archaeological discovery made by the North American anthropologist Johan Reinhard and the Peruvian mountaineer Miguel Zarate, in 1995, in the snowy Ampato, near the city of Arequipa. They found an Inca mummy in a perfect state of preservation. It was an adolescent girl of approximately 12 to 15 years of age, who was called the "Ice Maiden" or the "Juanita" mummy.

At the four ends of Chachabamba, there are four groups of ceremonial fountains in the number of three. These must have been used for purification ceremonies. Approximately five or six years ago, local archaeologists found in the upper part of this complex some canals that supplied water to these fountains.

The type of architecture in Chachabamba is of simple architecture, with carved stone masonry, not polished, and joined with mud mortar. Except for the enclosure that protects the main altar, whose architecture is made of carved stone blocks joined without mud mortar, so it must have been the most important

CHAPTER VIII THE SHORT INCA TRAIL TO MACHU PICCHU (2 DAYS-1 NIGHT)

Chachabamba was a ceremonial center on the road to Machu Picchu.

construction of the site, also because of its location near the Urubamba River.

The Inca complex of Chachabamba, by the characteristics that it presents as a whole, must have been a site of religious character on the way to the Inca city. The site was abandoned upon the arrival of the Spaniards to be discovered in the mid-twentieth century.

After visiting Chachabamba, you will walk through a ravine where a small river flows. From this place, the hiker will begin to climb the mountain. The hike is uphill, with steps and small flat places. From the valley floor to the Wiñawayna complex, there is a variety of fauna and flora such as orchids, begonias, or bromeliads. To the right side, we have a fantastic view of the Urubamba River.

The best way to enjoy this hike is: "take it easy, hold your llamas" or "slow but sure". At one hour, you have a small resting place, or refuge, where you can see the apu Veronica, which is the highest mountain in the Urubamba range, being also the most important in the Sacred Valley of the Incas.

Forty minutes later, we arrive at another refuge, from where we can see another Inca complex, very close to the Urubamba River called Choquesuysuy.

Choquesuysuy

The Choquesuysuy archeological site is located on the left bank of the Urubamba River and the left bank of the Phuyupatamarka stream, at km. 106 of the railroad line. Its ecological floor is the high jungle and its UTM coordinates are:

East	North	Altitude (masl and feet)
767602	8540813.3	2,163/7,095

In 1915, Choquesuysuy was discovered by the assistant surveyor Clarence Maynard, from the famous expedition of Hiram Bingham, who gave it the name of Choquesuysuy.

The Choquesuysuy archaeological complex is located on the left bank of the Urubamba River.

CHAPTER VIII THE SHORT INCA TRAIL TO MACHU PICCHU (2 DAYS-1 NIGHT)

This complex, at the time of its discovery, was completely covered by vegetation. In 1941, on the occasion of the expedition led by Paul Fejos, Dr. Axel Wenner Gren carried out exploration and vegetation clearing works, staying there for a month, and carrying out the topographic and photographic survey of the site.

That same year, the North American archaeologist Dr. Jhon H. Rowe carried out archaeological excavations, finding Inca-style ceramic fragments that correspond to pots, stone hammers, spinning wheels, and metallic elements, such as knives.

In 1987, anthropologist Fidel Ramos Condori carried out restoration work on Choquesuysuy for its protection and preservation. It is still preserved by the Ministry of Culture.

Based on the archaeological evidence, its geographic location near Machu Picchu, the type of engineering, as well as the fact that it is built around a hillside, we can indicate that it must have served several functions:

Choquesuysuy was a ceremonial and agricultural center and a tampu.

1. Choquesuysuy could have been a resting place, or tampu, on the way to the Inca city, as it has many enclosures that could have served as dwellings.
2. This site could have been a ceremonial center, due to the presence of many *pacchas*, or water fountains, which were very well worked in its architecture. Nearby there is a waterfall where water cults must have been performed.
3. Choquesuysuy, as a whole, has a large number of agricultural terraces that must have been used for the cultivation of coca leaf, cassava, corn, corn, chili, and some fruits such as *pacae*, the same that must have supplied Machu Picchu or the Urubamba valley. There is also the presence of qollqas, which were used to store the crops.

There is a road that connects to the Inca complex of Chachabamba, at the level of the valley floor, as well as there must have been another route that connected to Machu Picchu.

From Choquesuysuy, there is an Inca road that would connect with the Wiñaywayna complex. This must have been the original road, but not the one from Chachabamba to Wiñaywayna. The original road is today covered with vegetation.

From the second resting place, thirty-five minutes away, there is an incredible view of the Wiñaywayna complex. The question arises: How could the Incas build this site in this place, on the side of a mountain, in the jungle? The answer is found as you reach the city of Machu Picchu.

Before arriving at Wiñaywayna, there is a large waterfall whose waters come down from the mountains of the Phuyupatamarca sector where there is a complex of the same name. This

Wiñaywayna waterfalls are located ten minutes before reaching Wiñaywayna.

is a great place to take pictures, make videos and listen to the singing of the water.

Ten minutes away is Wiñawayna, which we have already described in the previous chapter[11]. When you reach this site, you go up some small steps and around the corner, there is an open rectangular enclosure, which must have served as a resting place or entrance control. From this place, in the lower part, you can observe the system of agricultural terraces, with carved stone masonry joined with mud mortar, and the steep steps that lead to the upper part, where the urban and religious sectors are located.

After exploring this great Inca complex, and before leaving, the hiker can take a very different photo and admire the majesty of the site. You will be able to understand its mystery.

The archaeological complex of Wiñaywayna must have been "the last spiritual resting place" towards the Inca city of Machu Picchu.

---

11   See chapter VII, pp. 100-103.

CHAPTER VIII THE SHORT INCA TRAIL TO MACHU PICCHU (2 DAYS-1 NIGHT)

Wiñaywayna is the most beautiful Inca complex before reaching the sacred citadel.

As we had already indicated in the previous chapter, from the Wiñaywayna camp to the Inti Punku site it is an hour and even a little more of walking. It is a smoother trail with small ascents and descents, linking like the original Inca trail leading to Machu Picchu. This part of the trail should be walked very slowly because in some places the road is quite dangerous.

The most outstanding thing you can see in the bottom of the Urubamba valley, the path that makes the same river in the form of a snake, which in the time of the Incas considered the Urubamba River as the milky way, where you could see the constellations and mainly the constellation of the Southern Cross, as well as the majesty of the apu Veronica.

Before arriving at Inti Punku you have the famous "matador de gringos" which is a large number of very steep steps so that the hiker to see them feels very helpless to climb them. But with desire and a lot of energy, it is possible to climb them, and at the end of

THE INCA TRAIL TO MACHU PICCHU

these steps, there is a small viewpoint that must have been used in Inca times, as a place of control of the Inca trail to the citadel.

Twelve more minutes of walking and you arrive at the Puerta del Sol, or Inti Punku, from *inti*, the sun, and *punku*, door. For a more precise description of Inti Punku, the reader is of course referred to the previous chapter[12].

Inti Punku, the Sun Gate, also called *Arcopongo*.

From this place, as the hiker gets closer to Machu Picchu, he has a great view and can realize how big the Inca city is.

The advantage of this trek with the famous Inca Trail of four days and three nights is that the hiker will have the opportunity to be in Machu Picchu twice: day one **and day two. For people who do not have a lot of time available, this is the most recommendable formulas.**

From the citadel of Machu Picchu to the town of Aguas Calientes, our overnight stay, the hiker will have two options: by bus (25 minutes of travel), or on foot (one hour and ten minutes of walking).

Aguas Calientes is also known as "Machu Picchu Pueblo". It is a small town in the high jungle, located on the right bank of the

---

12   See chapter VII, pp. 104-105.

CHAPTER VIII THE SHORT INCA TRAIL TO MACHU PICCHU (2 DAYS-1 NIGHT)

View of Machu Picchu and the Urubamba valley from Inti Punku.

Urubamba River, at an altitude of 2,040 meters/6,691 feet. It is a town that offers various tourist services, such as hotels, restaurants, bars, discos, laundries, and other services. At the top are the thermal baths. The estimated population as of the 2017 census is 5,347 inhabitants, making it one of the most peaceful towns in Peru! And you will almost feel at home!

Day 2 - Let's explore the citadel of Machu Picchu

From the town of Aguas Calientes to the Inca city of Machu Picchu, as on the first day, you have two options: by bus or on foot. If the hiker is planning to walk from the town of Aguas Calientes to the city of Machu Picchu, he/she will have to get up very early. We recommend leaving your accommodation no later than 4:00 am.

For this reason you will need to bring a flashlight because you will be walking in the dark. From the town of Aguas Calientes to

Descending from Inti Punku to Machu Picchu.

"Puentes Ruinas" it takes twenty-five minutes of walking, having to wait in line because there is an entrance control. This control opens at 5:00 am. After the control, cross the bridge and then take the road to the right, where there is a sign, and then ascend to Machu Picchu.

This tour takes forty to fifty minutes, or a little more, depending on your physical condition. It is a small marathon. In some sections, there are very high steps. Then, when you arrive at the Machu Picchu control point, generally the hiker arrives very tiredly and sweaty. Therefore, we recommend wearing a clean and dry polo shirt to visit the citadel.

Recommendations before visiting Machu Picchu :

1. Use the restrooms, as there will be no restrooms available during the visit.
2. If the hiker has a backpack of more than twenty-five liters, it will have to be stored in the cloakroom, as it is not allowed

CHAPTER VIII THE SHORT INCA TRAIL TO MACHU PICCHU (2 DAYS-1 NIGHT)

to be carried inside the citadel. Only small backpacks of 20 liters maximum are allowed.
3. For the visit to Machu Picchu, bring your original passport; show your student card if you have one, and your Inca Trail ticket.
4. Carry in your backpack bottles (glass or metal) of water, snacks such as cookies or energy bars, keeping the garbage in your pocket or backpack.
5. Dress comfortably, since Machu Picchu is located in the high jungle and there are two seasons (rainy and dry), sunglasses, caps, hats, rain ponchos if necessary, sunblock, mosquito repellent.

You are ready to visit Machu Picchu!

Classic place where the traditional photo is taken.

THE INCA TRAIL TO MACHU PICCHU

CHAPTER IX
MACHU PICCHU, INCA CITY

To explain or talk about Machu Picchu would take us an infinite number of chapters. Today, a multitude of books explain in detail what was the Inca citadel. Specialized books about its history, its architecture, or its construction system. Machu Picchu remains and will remain a source of wonder and mystery. Under its vegetation and underground, new enigmas still await the archaeologists of the future.

Today, the visit to the Inca citadel is regulated by the Ministry of Culture, an institution that from time to time introduces new rules or provisions, with the idea of preserving the site for future generations.

Since the recent measures aimed at better controlling the flow of tourists, three circuits have been enabled: a short, a medium, and a long, this also according to the availability of time that tourists have. Also, according to the new disposition of the government, the Inca citadel can only be visited *once*. If you want to visit it again, you will have *to* buy a new entrance ticket. This is the reason why we always advise tourists, as far as possible, to opt for the long tour.

Inca city of Machu Picchu. The sacred city.

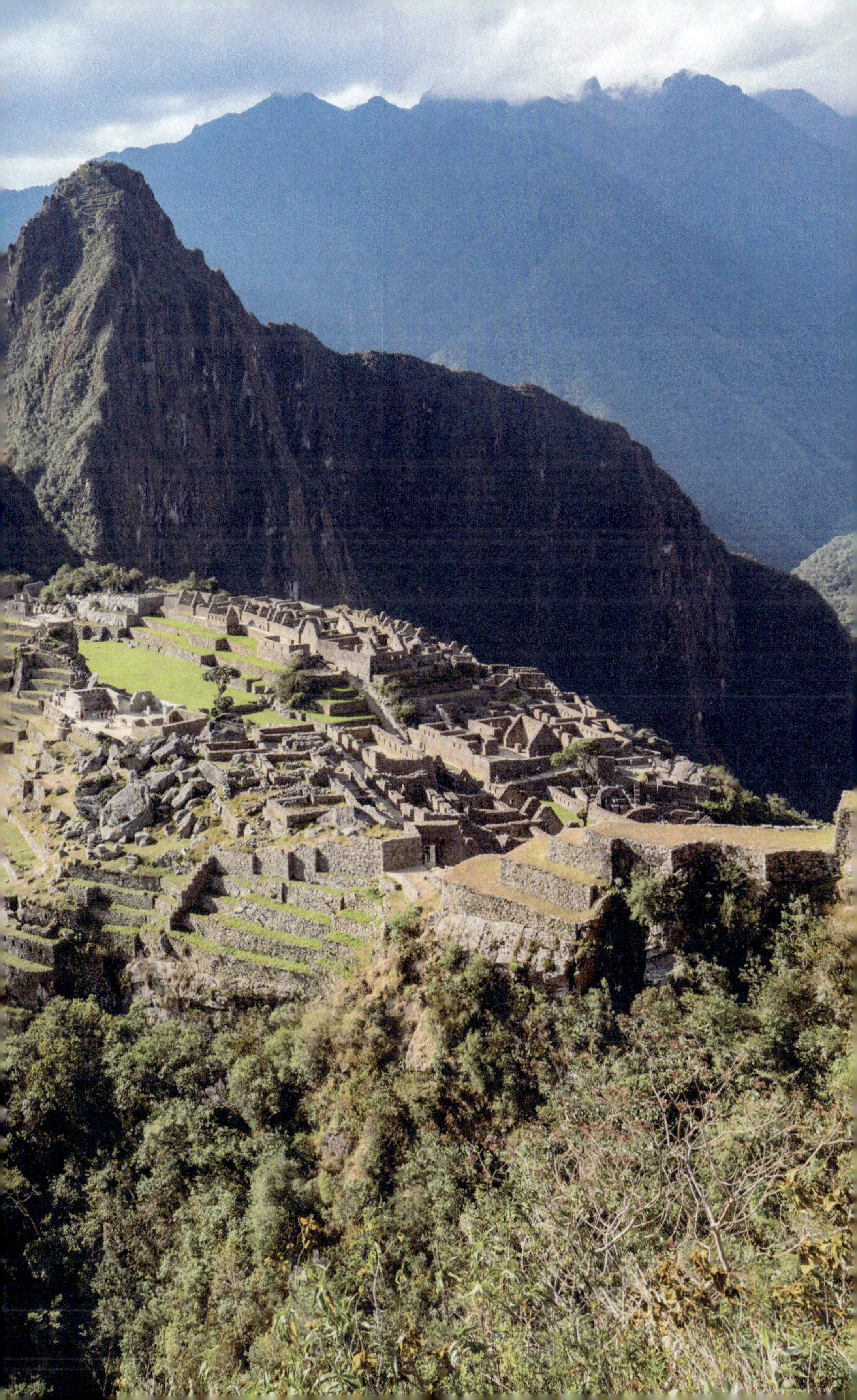

In this sense, we recommend the tourist to[13] take the path to the left side, and the steps above. This will take about twelve to fifteen minutes and you will arrive at the classic place, from where the best pictures of Machu Picchu are taken. This point is easy to locate since most tourists take their "selfies" from there.

But if you want an even better photo, I recommend that you go a little further up to the "Casa de los Guardianes" (House of the Guardians). It is an isolated building with a thatched roof, overlooking a large part of the Inca citadel. From here, the panorama is fantastic! Photographs taken, we are ready to explore Machu Picchu.

The search for Machu Picchu

The Inca city was officially discovered by the American explorer Hiram Bingham on July 24, 1911.

But Bingham was not looking for this site, but the lost city of Vilcabamba, which was the last refuge of the Incas, after Cusco, capital of the Tawantinsuyo, was destroyed and sacked by the Spaniards. The same fate befell small cities such as Pisac, Ollantaytambo, as well as important ceremonial sites, where the conquerors looted the most valuable ceremonial paraphernalia, after melting them down and sending them to the king of Spain in the form of ingots.

It is important to remember that, at the end of the 16th century and the beginning of the 17th century, the kingdom of Spain was the richest and most powerful in Europe and the world. A few years before the conquest of the Inca empire, the Aztec and Mayan cultures in Mexico and Central America were subdued by Hernán Cortez in 1519 and 1524. Eight years later, in 1532, Fran-

---

13   This, after storing your personal clothing in the cloakroom, using the restrooms, and passing the main checkpoint a minute's walk away.

CHAPTER IX: MACHU PICCHU, INCA CITY

cisco Pizarro, after several attempts, managed to conquer the Tawantinsuyo.

The Spaniards, after destroying and plundering all the places that had gold and silver, had the idea of introducing a new culture (language, religion, European customs), taking the farmlands, and starting to kill the local inhabitants, especially those who resisted being subdued by the Spanish yoke, added to the introduction of new epidemics that killed thousands of the Incas.

When he assumed supposedly as the new Inca, after the very ephemeral Paullu Inca, Manco II, in 1537, and seeing the mistreatment, abuse, and destruction that the Spaniards were committing in Cusco and many other places, he decided to take up arms. With the idea of regaining control of the government and evict the invaders, he made the first rebellion against the conquerors from the heights of Cusco. But Manco Inca was finally defeated by the Spaniards, who received help from many local ethnic groups, dissatisfied with the Inca government.

Manco had to retreat to the Sacred Valley and the site of Ollantaytambo, this place being for a time a town of resistance. However, they were also defeated by the invaders. Manco Inca, then, had to retreat to the last Inca refuge called Vilcabamba, in the wild north of the department of Cusco. In this process of escape, the heir of the Inca emperors commanded to destroy the roads leading to the city of Machu Picchu. Likewise, he ordered to burn the main qollqas that were located along the Urubamba River, in order not to supply his enemies.

A clear example is the classic four-day Inca trail. From the Runkuraqay complex, you can see an important part of the original trail used by Manco II to Machu Picchu. However, after 1537, the city of Vilcabamba became the last refuge of the Incas.

They were thirty-five years of desperate resistance against the Spaniards. But, in 1572, the conquerors managed to locate Vilcabamba, thanks to the help of the information provided by the priests and the local people. Thus, like Cusco, Vilcabamba was sacked and destroyed by the Spaniards. The last descendant of the Incas, the young Tupac Amaru, was captured and then taken back to Cusco in chains. He was executed a few days later in the Plaza de Armas. Thus ended the dynasty of the Sapa Incas.

Hiram Bingham's idea was to find this last refuge of Inca dissidence. With the help of Peruvian, governmental, and local authorities, he organized the famous "Yale Expedition" in search of the lost city of Vilcabamba. On July 22nd, 1911, on his journey from the town of Ollantaytambo to the high jungle, along the bridle path on the right bank of the Urubamba River, he discovered several Inca complexes such as Salapunku, Qhanabamba, Q'entimarka, Qoriwayrachina, Patawasi, Paucarcancha, and other sites.

The following day, taking the bridle path, Hiram Bingham passed through the sites of Pampacahua, Cedrobamba, and Makiñayuq, today is known as Aguas Calientes, arriving in the afternoon, to the sector called Mandorpampa. Today, this site is located one or two hours walking following the railroad line from Aguas Calientes. Following the route of the Urubamba River, in the direction of the sector called Hidroeléctrica, establishing as a base camp, Bingham met the local settler called Melchor Arteaga, who lived in that place cultivating sugar cane and corn.

With the help of Sergeant Carrasco, the American explorer established a conversation with Arteaga. When he asked him if there were Inca ruins in this place, the peasant told him that on the top of the mountain, which they called Machu Picchu, there were many ruins, with a large number of terraces from the Inca period.

Nowadays, many adventurers, explorers, or archaeologists discover archaeological evidence, because it is the peasants who, when carrying out the activity of "rose and burn", cause fires to clear their fields of vegetation and when they are unable to control them, they cause large fires. The other thing is when the local inhabitants, in their daily work of looking for better pastures for their cattle, manage to discover ruins. When the explorers ask the locals if in their walks through some areas they saw ancient constructions, and when they share with them some liquor, coca leaves and offer them some money, the villagers open their mouths, being able to explain in detail the exact places where these ruins are and also explain what they are going to find. This is how Hiram Bingham discovers the Inca city of Machu Picchu.

Discovery Day

On July 24th, 1911, in the morning hours, guided by Melchor Arteaga and accompanied by Sergeant Carrasco, who was security provided by the Peruvian government, Hiram Bingham left Mandorpampa, with the Urubamba River and the Huayna Picchu mountain on his right side.

After walking for about an hour, they arrived where the place called Puente Ruinas is now located. For tourists wishing to go up from the town of Aguas Calientes to Machu Picchu on foot, there is a checkpoint. There was then a small bridge made with tied sticks, where they had to cross the Urubamba River from one bank to the other, having to take a path that is still used today.

This road must have been the one that links Chachabamba with Choquesuysuy and from there to Machu Picchu, climbing it uphill[14]. At the end of this hike, they met where today is the Belmond Sanctuary Lodge tourist hotel.

Hiram Bingham, Sergeant Carrasco, and Melchor Arteaga met two peasant families with small houses made of stones and thatched roofs, Anacleto Alvarez and Toribio Recharte, who was known to Melchor Arteaga.

Several years before Bingham, the Inca city had already been occupied by local peasants; in fact, Machu Picchu was already known by the locals who lived on the floor of the Urubamba valley. Likewise, it was already inhabited on the outskirts by peasant families, who continued to use the Inca agricultural terraces as small spaces for the cultivation of corn. There would be one or more questions: Was Machu Picchu discovered or rediscovered? Yes, Machu Picchu was already known, explored, and visited by local people. These people could have found in the Inca citadel quite a lot of archaeological evidence. What did they do with it? We leave those questions there. However, Machu Picchu was also looted at the end of the 19th century by the German Augusto Burns and President Cacéres. Both created a joint venture whose main activity was the looting of the site and the sale of the archaeological material found to foreign collectors...

Finally, Hiram Bingham discovered Machu Picchu in the name of science. He established contact with the local families. They gave him their attention as a visitor. In the Andean culture, when someone visits a local family for the first time, they provide a small meal and a drink. This custom is still practiced in the Peruvian Andes.

---

14 This road must have been used by local people already living in Machu Picchu when they wished to descend to the valley floor of the Urubamba River.

CHAPTER IX: MACHU PICCHU, INCA CITY

After taking a break, Bingham was accompanied by one of the sons of these families, named Pablito, who together with Sergeant Carrasco began the first exploration of Machu Picchu.

We could say that the boy Pablito, was the first local guide, who guided a tourist in the Inca citadel. After walking for a couple of minutes, Hiram Bingham must have seen in front of him large constructions that were covered with vegetation. And when he passed where the qollqas sector is now, he must have been surprised with such a discovery of a complete city, hidden in the jungle.

While touring Machu Picchu, Bingham must have been very surprised to see the kind of fine architecture that can be seen today in the temples of the Sun or the Three Windows, in the Main Temple and the famous Intiwatana, and then understand how great the city of Machu Picchu was.

At the end of this first exploration, the Yale explorer had to descend to the valley floor by the same route and then head for his camp in the Mandorpampa area.

This is how Hiram Bingham found Machu Picchu, giving him the title of "scientific discoverer" because thanks to Hiram Bingham the whole world was made aware of the existence of this great wonder of the world.

The following year, in 1912, Hiram Bingham organized the next expedition, called "The Peruvian Expedition Auspices of the Yale University and the National Geographic Society". It was conformed by a team of professional people such as George Eaton, Robert Stepheson, Paul Bestor, Albert H. Bunsteat, Herverd E. Gregory, Elwood C. Erdis, Luther T. Nelson, and Osgood Hardy. The Peruvian president at that time was Augusto B. Leguía, who offered him the facilities for the scientific study of the city. He also gave him the exclusive concession for the project.

It was four months of hard work, cleaning vegetation, for which they had to hire the villagers who lived on the floor of the Urubamba River valley, as well as the local farmers, Toribio Recharte and Anacleto Álvarez. While doing this work, the workers must have encountered many poisonous snakes or vipers, so in some sectors, they had to use fire to clean the enclosures.

At the end of this work, Hiram Bingham carried out several excavations in the precincts of the Main Temple and the Temple of the Three Windows, in which he made the first photographic record. The scientific expedition must have found a lot of archaeological evidence such as ceramics, metallurgy, and funerary contexts. Many of these finds were taken to Yale University, which was one of the sponsors of this expedition.

Today, if you want to see the best findings made by Hiram Bingham, you have to visit the private collections of Yale University in the United States. At present, near the place called Puente Ruinas, there is a site museum called "Museo Inca Manuel Chávez Ballón", in honor of the first local archaeologist, who did a lot of archaeological work in the city of Cusco and Machu Picchu. In this museum, you can see various archaeological evidence, such as ceramics, metallurgy, lithics, and bones. However, after Bingham's discovery, at present, the Peruvian government as well as international organizations, continue to carry out scientific research work, for which you must have a very special permit, given by the Ministry of Culture.

CHAPTER IX: MACHU PICCHU, INCA CITY

After this initial clearing of vegetation and excavation work, a sectorization was carried out and the most important constructions were named, some of which, over time, have taken another name.

Let's visit the city of Machu Picchu

Now it is time to explore Machu Picchu. We will depart from the sector of the *House of the Guardians*.

House of the Guardians

In this place, there is a single enclosure covered with a thatched roof, which must have served as a control point of the Inca city. Near it, there is an usnhu where ceremonies or llama sacrifices could have taken place. From the House of the Guardians, the entire citadel can be observed. Behind it is the mountain of Huayna Picchu, and even farther away from the surrounding mountains. At the bottom of the valley meanders the Urubamba River that

Machu Picchu, the *House of the Guardians*. From this point, you can see the entire Inca city.

descends in the direction of the Hidroelectrica sector. This point is a great place to take a personal, group, or family photos.

As one descends into the Inca city, the tourist will have several places from which to continue taking good pictures. When you reach the second corner, there is usually a government guard in uniform with a whistle. It is in this place where most tourists take their group and personal photos.

Following the main road to the left side, you will see a large gate of more detailed architecture, which must have been in Inca times, the main gate of access to Machu Picchu. But before crossing this gate, you have the agricultural sector.

The agricultural sector

In Inca times, all large and small llaqtas were divided into three sectors: agricultural, religious, and urban. The agricultural sector is located at this level since there are a large number of terraces on the outskirts of the city. They must have cultivated

Machu Picchu, agricultural sector. The cultivation terraces were built on the mountainside.

corn, yucca, sweet potato, chili, aguaymanto, and especially coca leaf.

The same that should have supplied the inhabitants of Machu Picchu, although it would not be enough. Let's remember that there are places near the citadel that must have supplied other agricultural products, such as the complexes of Intipata, Wiñaywayna, Choquesuysuy, Qoriwayrachina, and others. In this sector, there are also several qollqas that are currently well preserved and covered with thatched roofs, where the crops of different products must have been stored.

Crossing the main gate, we enter the Inca city. After the first enclosure, to the right side, there are a large number of rectangular-shaped, large, two-story dwellings, which must have been kallankas. These buildings may have served to house a large number of people or families who came to Machu Picchu for the biggest festivals of the Inca calendar, such as the Inti Raymi, on the

Machu Picchu. The qollqas were the constructions where the crops were stored.

occasion of the winter solstice, on June 21st, or the Capac Raymi, during the summer solstice, on December 22nd.

These people came from all over Tawantinsuyo. Each ethnic group, or group of people, should have been well dressed and bringing the most important offerings from their place of origin. An example would be if the group of people coming from the Sacred Valley could have brought as offering corn, the main product grown in this area. Those coming from present-day Ecuador, where the Galapagos Islands are located, could have brought as an offering the famous mullu, the spondylus, or seashells, an offering highly appreciated in Inca times for representing the element of water.

A few dozen meters after the main entrance, here is the *"Temple of the Three Gates"*.

The Temple of the Three Gates

The Three Gates enclosure is located before descending to the quarry sector.

This enclosure is very important. In April 2012, the Inkarri Cusco Institute conducted a surface archaeological research work, duly authorized by the Ministry of Culture. This was called the *"Surface Archaeological Research Project (without excavation) in the Inca citadel of Machu Picchu"*. It had as members for its execution the following people: the Archaeologist Hilbert Sumire Bustincio, as Director of the Research Project, the French-Peruvian researcher Thierry Jamin, as Executive Director and President of the Inkarri Institute, the French Engineer David Crespi, José Casafranca Montes, Vice-president of the same institute, and Spanish Archaeologist Daniel Merino Panizo, a specialist in archaeolo-

CHAPTER IX: MACHU PICCHU, INCA CITY

Machu Picchu. Location of the enclosure of the Three Gates.

gical sites in a funerary context, and the cameraman, Edward Valenzuela Gil, Responsible for Public Relations at the institute.

In April 2010, David Crespi visited the city of Machu Picchu. That year, the department of Cusco had problems with the weather. Many spots of rain caused the difficulty of entry and exit to Aguas Calientes, since most tourists arrive at this town by rail. And the torrential rains had destroyed part of the railway. Thousands of tourists were stranded in Aguas Calientes and the authorities were trying to evacuate them gradually by helicopter to Cusco. So, while waiting to be evacuated, David Crespy went several times to visit Machu Picchu.

Thus, one day, while touring and exploring the Inca citadel, he discovered a very strange doorway, or access opening, at the base of one of the most imposing buildings of Machu Picchu: the

Machu Picchu. Under the enclosure of the Three Gates is located the access to the funerary context.

CHAPTER IX: MACHU PICCHU, INCA CITY

Temple of the Three Gates. This prompted him to ask the park rangers if this mysterious covered entrance had been studied or if any archaeological research had been carried out, which caused the park rangers to be puzzled and they could not answer David.

This prompted the French tourist, upon returning to his country, to send several emails to the Ministry of Culture so that the people in charge of the Historic Sanctuary of Machu Picchu could provide some kind of information about the cover. Unfortunately, he did not receive any kind of response or message.

Then, David Crespi, made contact with the researcher Thierry Jamin, after reading an article in the French magazine "Le Figaro Magazine", dedicated to the investigations that the French explorer was carrying out in the area of the National Sanctuary of Megantoni about the traces of Paititi, the famous lost city of the Incas. Jamin visited Machu Picchu several times to investigate this "entrance". Thus, in December 2011, the Inkarri Institute presented a research project to the Ministry of Culture, whose objective was to carry out several electromagnetic surveys to try to locate the presence of subway chambers in the subsoil of the Temple of the Three Gates and thus confirm the doubts of David Crespy. On May 22nd, 2012, this project was approved and authorized for execution.

In April 2012, the Inkarri Institute conducted multiple archaeological surveys at Machu Picchu, using several georadars to study the subsoil of the citadel. Among others, the GOLDEN KING DPRP 3D, the Molecular Frequency Discriminator, the ROVER CII New Edition, and the CAVEFINDER. This survey work was carried out under the supervision of the Director of the Historic Sanctuary of Machu Picchu, anthropologist Fernando Astete Victoria and an army of resident archaeologists, such as archaeologist Piedad

Champi, or archaeologists Werner Delgado and Rolando Alegria.

The members of the Inkarri Institute, under the technical direction of Engineer Ricardo Tamaki Hamada, first located a possible cavity, or tomb, because the GOLDEN KING DPRP 3D equipment and the Molecular Frequency Discriminator detected a passage, or corridor, in a northwest direction. This access, several meters long, had an estimated initial depth of 2.10 meters, where it showed a staggering tiered tier in the number of five tiers. The GOLDEN KING also detected the presence of several metal objects inside probable niches. By their red, orange, and yellow coloration, these mysterious objects indicated a non-ferrous composition, i.e. gold or silver.

Machu Picchu. Archaeologist Hilbert Sumire, director of the Archaeological Project, and Thierry Jamin, President of the Inkarri Cusco Institute.

Other equipment was also used, such as the ROVER CII New Edition and the CAVEFINDER, confirming not only the corridor detected by Ricardo Tamaki a few days earlier, but also the presence of a large quadrangular-shaped room, three meters on each side, and a dozen human-sized cavities. According to the analysis of the two companies contracted by the Inkarri Institute to carry out these resonances, the doubt was not possible: it was an important funerary context of the Inca period, belonging, according to all verisimilitude, to an important personage of the Tawantinsuyo. The probably located tombs undoubtedly belonged to a key figure of the Inca society (perhaps the emperor Pachacúteq himself, founder of Machu Picchu) and his panaka, that is to say, to his lineage. Three of these tombs, located in the southern part of the temple, seemed to belong to young children.

Finally, the presence of large non-ferrous metal deposits (gold and silver) associated with most of the cavities seems to confirm the presence, in the subsoil of the Templo de las Tres Portadas, of a funerary context of the first magnitude...[15]

Machu Picchu. Using the resonance equipment with the Golden King DPRP 3D.

The reason for this finding, it was suggested that this cavity could have been the tomb, or mausoleum, of the Inca Pachacuteq, and it was hypothesized that the physical body (his mummy) of the great Sapa Inca could be found.

However, some chronicles diverge on this point. According to Juan de Betanzos, the mummy of Pachacuteq was still in its "Patallacta", the original name of Machu Picchu, around 1551. However, a few years later, in 1569, Polo de Ondegardo affirms that the conquerors would have discovered the remains of the

---

15 See the important article published in 2016 in the prestigious American magazine, Forbes, on this research: https://www.forbes.com/sites/jimdobson/2016/07/26/will-a-hidden-treasure-chamber-discovered-under-machu-picchu-finally-be-revealed/?sh=77972be05d8d

Machu Picchu. The Director of the Sanctuary of Machu Picchu, Anthropologist Fernando Astete Victoria, supervises the archaeological research project.

emperor in Cusco, in the sector of Tokocachi (the current district of San Blas), then sent to Lima to the viceroy of Cañete, accompanied by several other mummified bodies of rulers.

The mummies of the Inca emperors were later hidden in a secret crypt of the current San Andres hospital, where they are still believed to be.

However, one question remains: would the Incas have taken the crazy risk of bringing back to Cusco the most revered of the Inca mummies knowing that the Spaniards were doing everything possible to find her? That does not make sense. Thus, for almost five centuries, the debate remains...

The mummy of Pachacuteq may no longer be in his mausoleum today. This is another debate. But the important thing is that the most problematic hypothesis remains that the Temple of the Three Gates was indeed the mausoleum of the emperor

CHAPTER IX: MACHU PICCHU, INCA CITY

Pachacúteq, founder of Tawantinsuyo.

Thanks to David Crespy, this finding would be very important, since, in Peruvian archaeology, the physical body of an Inca Sapac has never been found, and imagining that the mummy of Pachacuteq could be found increases these expectations. For that, the city of Machu Picchu keeps in its geographical context, many archaeological pieces of evidence that wait to be discovered by the archaeologists of

Machu Picchu. Using the Golden King DPRP 3D, with the "medium plate", in the access shaft of the funerary context.

the future. For more details about this incredible discovery, do not hesitate to visit this website: www.machupicchu-ciudadela.com.[16]

When this discovery was made, following the protocols of the Ministry of Culture and modern archaeology, the *Final Report* of the project was presented, receiving a few months later the "approval" of the Peruvian authorities.

A few weeks later, the Inkarri Institute team presented a new research project to the Ministry of Culture, whose objectives will be to open the entrance discovered by David Crespy, as well as to study the archaeological material detected inside the subway cavities located by the penetration radars.

---

16 Also, see the book in French by Thierry Jamin, entitled «Machu Picchu et la chambre secrète», éd. Jungle Doc Productions, France, mars 2020.

Unfortunately, local officials of the Ministry of Culture will generate great controversy. And even the Inkarri Institute will receive anonymous death threats. It seems that this incredible discovery generated a lot of jealousy on the part of certain officials in charge of the Historic Sanctuary of Machu Picchu and the Dirección Desconcentrada de Cultura Cusco (DDC-Cusco). At least that is the opinion of the famous Peruvian archaeologist Federico Kauffmann Doig in his two-volume book, dedicated to Machu Picchu and published in November 2013[17].

Machu Picchu. The Golden King DPRP 3D team. Shows the discovery in the Temple of the *Three Gates*.

Because of these controversies, the Ministry of Culture will not authorize the Inkarri Institute to proceed with the opening of the mysterious entrance. This issue of the probable "mausoleum of the emperor Pachacuteq" had become political. In 2014, after months of negotiations with the authorities, the Inkarri Institute decided to give up this project. To this day, the mysterious entrance discovered in 2010 at the foot of the Temple of the Three Gates remains closed. But for how much longer?

---

17 See the article written by Federico Kauffmann Doig in his book, entitled, «La tumba de Pachacútec: ¿en Machu Picchu?», Vol. 02, pp. 702-703.

CHAPTER IX: MACHU PICCHU, INCA CITY

As a member of the Instituto Inkarri Cusco and director of this archaeological project, I can attest to the seriousness and great professionalism of the Instituto Inkarri. Created in Cusco in 2009, its main purpose is the study of the permanent presence of the Incas in the Peruvian Amazon, besides having respect and love for this great Inca culture. As a professional archaeologist from the city of Cusco, I am outraged by the dishonest behavior and lack of professional ethics of these third-rate officials and I am convinced that history will judge them very severely.

From 2012 to the present year, 2020, this enclosure has been closed to the visit of tourists who want to know what this place hides. It will be the Ministry of Culture of Cusco, with local archaeologists at its service, in charge of opening the tomb in the future and thus show the whole world the secret hidden in these mysterious cavities.

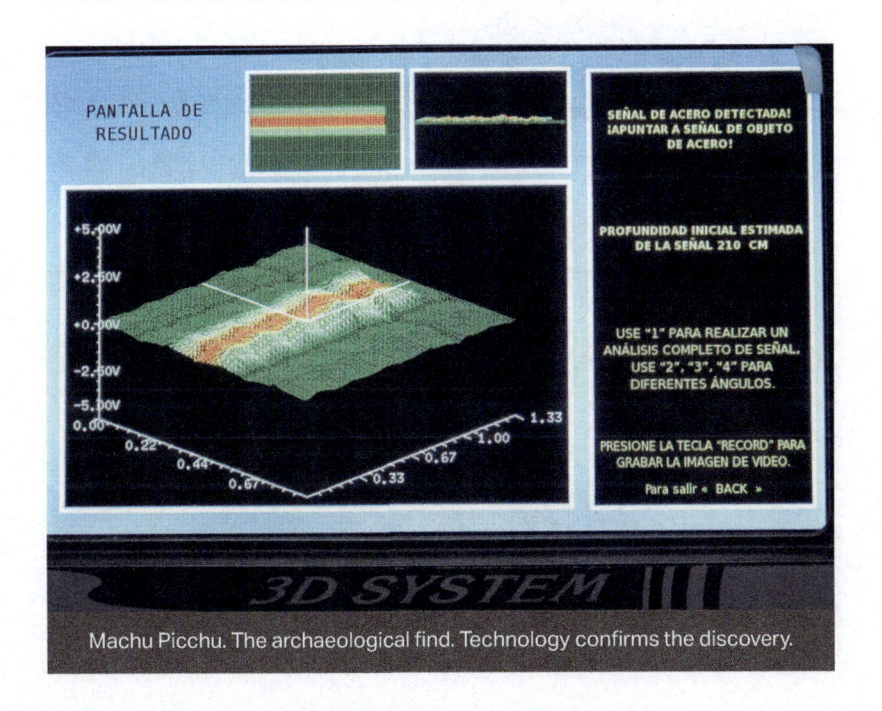

Machu Picchu. The archaeological find. Technology confirms the discovery.

THE INCA TRAIL TO MACHU PICCHU

Before descending to the quarry area, on the left side, there is a great viewpoint from where tourists can have an incredible view of Machu Picchu and the Huayna Picchu mountain.

When descending the steps, follow the sign (arrow) to the right side, which will lead you to the Temple of the Sun, which can be observed inside the temple from the top.

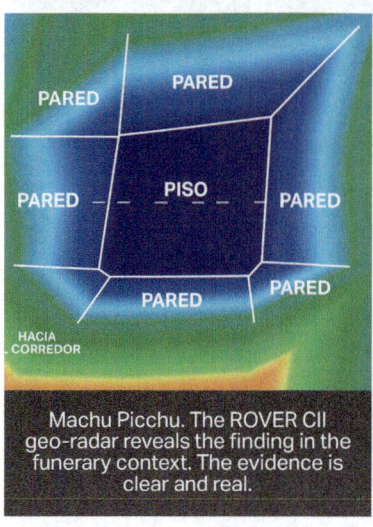

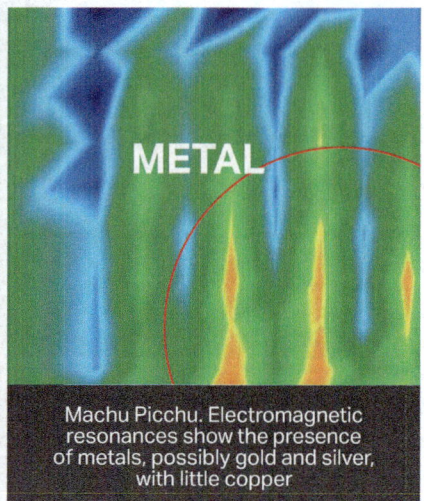

Machu Picchu. Use of ROVER CII equipment, New Edition.

Machu Picchu. The ROVER CII geo-radar reveals the finding in the funerary context. The evidence is clear and real.

Machu Picchu. Electromagnetic resonances show the presence of metals, possibly gold and silver, with little copper

234

CHAPTER IX: MACHU PICCHU, INCA CITY

The Temple of the Sun

In 1912, when the explorer Hiram Bingham was studying Machu Picchu, he called this enclosure "the Tower", because this construction had the shape of a small tower but from a European vision. Thanks to later studies by archaeologists, this construction was renamed the Temple of the Sun.

This construction is located in the religious sector. His type of architecture is very fine, called *imperial architecture*, and dating from the time of Pachacuteq. This temple is built with well-carved stone masonry, joined without any mortar or mud mortar. The building was erected on a rock in situ, which must have been carved to place the masonry, giving it a semicircular shape. In its interior, small niches have been arranged to place offerings and idols.

The temple presents in its interior, in the central part, a small usnhu that must have been carved. The tower has two windows of regular size and a trapezoidal shape that are oriented to two very important points: the winter solstice, towards the San Gabriel mountain and the summer solstice, towards the Inti Punku. The window oriented towards the San Gabriel mountain has the temple of the Pachamama below.

During the winter solstice, the sun appears over the slope of the San Gabriel mountain, which has the shape of a "V" on its summit. This may have a natural shape, but it could have been carved by the Incas. That remains a question mark. If we compare it with the sector of Inti Punku, as a whole, the latter also has a "V" shape". In its middle part, we find the constructions, that is to say, in the middle between the mountain of Inti Punku and the mountain of Machu Picchu.

Machu Picchu and the *Temple of the Sun*. The left window is oriented towards the San Gabriel mountain, at the Winter solstice.

At the solstice, the sun, rising behind San Gabriel, upon reaching the top of the mountain, passes through the middle of the "V". Being very clear this observation, when the light crosses through the middle of this "V", the sun will illuminate the top of the Huayna Picchu Mountain, which has on its summit an usnhu, whose orientation is to the south, oriented towards Machu Picchu. Thus, we can understand why this citadel was a sacred and pilgrimage site at the time of the Incas. As the sun's rays gradually fall, then illuminate the Inca city, they will illuminate in particular the Temple of the Sun, the Temple of the Three Windows, and the famous Intiwatana.

The Temple of the Sun has two trapezoidal windows. One of them is oriented towards the San Gabriel mountain. Every June 21st, the first ray of sunlight passes through the middle of the window, illuminating an altar inside. This ray has a very bright rectangular shape, and then illuminates the entire enclosure and finally the entire city of Machu Picchu. This phenomenon can be observed days before or days after June 21st, for which we recommend visiting the citadel in the first shift of 6.00 am.

The second window, also trapezoidal, is oriented towards the Inti Punku. On December 22nd of each year, the phenomenon of the summer solstice takes place: It is the longest day of the year and the shortest night. The sun rises from the east point, with an orientation towards the apu Veronica. This phenomenon happens in the following way, in the area of Machu Picchu and its surroundings: the sun rises from the east side, illuminating the apu Veronica, which is the highest mountain in the Urubamba mountain range. As the sun rises from behind, the mountain blocks the rays that shine towards the western point, keeping Machu Picchu and its surroundings in shadow. But when the sun reaches the top of the Veronica, it will illuminate the mountain of Huayna Picchu, which has at its summit an altar facing south, and then the rays begin to descend towards the Inca citadel in the direction of the Intiwatana sector.

But at the same time that the sun rises and passes the top of the apu Veronica, the Inti Punku will be illuminated. Perhaps, for this reason, the Incas gave this construction the name of Puerta del Sol (Sun gate). After illuminating the Inti Punku, the sun's rays will illuminate one of the windows of the Temple of the Sun that is oriented to the east, towards the sector of the Inti Punku. When illuminating this temple, the first rays will pass through this window. Just like the window, which is oriented to the winter solstice, another very bright rectangular ray will be seen in the interior of this enclosure, in the upper part of the altar. At the same time that the sun will rise, it will pass through the top of the apu Veronica, and the Inti Punku will then be illuminated.

We must remember that in the Andes there are two seasons: the rainy season and the dry season. From October to April, we are in the wet season, where there is the presence of rains. However, the city of Machu Picchu is located in the high jungle, where clouds and fog are very frequent, especially in this season. If the weather conditions allow us to observe this phenomenon, which is contrary to the dry season from May to late September.

But we must understand that the Incas built their ceremonial observation centers (intiwatanas, temples of the Sun) throughout their territory, in the cities or small towns, to observe this phenomenon, the city of Machu Picchu not being the only place to observe it.

After examining the Temple of the Sun, the next place to visit is the House of the Inca. Towards the left side there is an Inca doorway that has an incredible view and whose background has the Huayna Picchu mountain, then descend, some steps and turn to the left side which is the entrance to the sector of the House of the Inca.

The House of the Inca

This building must have been occupied as the possible home of the Inca Pachacuteq during the time he stayed in the city of Machu Picchu: in times of rest or to celebrate very important festivities. The building has an imperial Inca style architecture, with stone masonry joined without mud mortar. However, it is clear to see at a certain height, a very different and simpler style or aestheticism. This is because this part has been restored for its preservation, since it is an open enclosure, without a roof, which in the rainy season is prone to have deteriorated.

In its interior, some niches must have been used to place domestic objects, such as small flat plates with flamebait to light up the room. On one side there is a separation that is observed at floor level, made by stones, and that must have been the place where the Inca slept, obviously with all the comforts and luxury of a sovereign. Alpaca skins may have been placed on the floor, and to cover himself with blankets made of vicuña wool. A bed made of tree trunks must have been placed in the enclosure.

Today, when visiting the peasant communities outside of Cusco, families sleep on the floor. They put a plastic sheet on top of it and place llama or alpaca skins on it. To cover themselves, they use blankets made of camelid or sheep wool, but if they have a little money they can buy modern blankets. Other families have modern beds or sometimes they can make their furniture made with tree trunks, placing mattresses made of ichu, wheat, or

CHAPTER IX: MACHU PICCHU, INCA CITY

barley straw at floor level, on top of it a thin cloth, which serves as a mattress cover and then places several blankets to protect themselves from the cold, especially in those places that are above 4,000 meters/13,120 feet.

In the sector of the House of the Inca, there is a patio in the central part, and in it, you can observe a carved rock that could have been used as small fulling mills to grind corn or other foods to prepare meals.

In front of the Inca's room, there is another rectangular room that could have been used for sleeping by the Inca's family, concubines, or other very important people.

Following the sign, we will get to another open rectangular patio, where there is a chamber, where archaeologists found fragments of pottery and llama bones, which could be offerings made to Pachamama, or Mother Nature. Following the route, we arrive at the sector of the Temple of Pachamama.

The Temple of Pachamama

This building is located below the Temple of the Sun. It is a construction made in situ, this means that before being worked, this

Machu Picchu. The Temple of Pachamama (or Mother Nature), is located below the Temple of the Sun

has been a small cave, carved little by little to build in its interior a great temple. Inside you can see that the wall on the right side was built with well-worked stone masonry. Here there are large trapezoidal niches, where the most important mummies or ceremonial paraphernalia (idols made of gold and silver) could have been placed. On the left side, the rock has been carved in

Machu Picchu. Main access gate to the *Temple of the Sun* and the *Temple of the Pachamama*.

the form of a double jamb, giving importance to this place. This temple has a very fine architecture.

In its interior, there is an altar, the same that was carved and polished, and possibly it should have served to be able to make observations in the winter solstice or to place some offerings. But what stands out is at the entrance of this construction. It is the carved rock that has the stepped sign in the form of gradients of three levels, which is very important in the Inca religion. It symbolizes the Andean world, it means that the "pata pata", gradients, which would mean the stepped sign. This would represent the power to communicate from one level to another, that is to say, from one ecological level to another. It would also come to be the representation of the *Andean trilogy*. It would represent the three worlds: the *Uju Pacha*, the *Kay Pacha*, and the *Hanan Pacha*, the same that would be represented by the sacred animals of the Incas: the snake, the puma, and the condor.

In Andean thought, each sacred animal represents a world. The Uju Pacha symbolizes the "world below". It is represented by the serpent, which would represent the rivers, streams, or the water element. It should be remembered that in Inca times, the main economy was agriculture, and the majority of the population were farmers. The Kay Pacha represents the "earthly world", where human beings lived and developed their lives. It is symbolized by the puma, which also represents power, cunning, and intelligence. The Hanan Pacha represents the "world above". It is represented by the condor, the sacred bird of the Andes, considered the messenger between humans and the apus. The condor is the only large bird that can fly above 7,000 meters (or 22,960 feet) and tell the Apus: "your children need water for their crops and pastures". The union of these three worlds together would represent the Pachamama or Mother Nature.

Continuing the tour, we now climb to the upper part of the citadel to visit the sector called Cantera (quarry).

The Quarry

The quarrying sector, or called by local archaeologists "geological chaos", has several examples of how the Incas extracted from the rock the stone blocks, which vary in size from small to large.

First, we must understand that all the mountains surrounding Machu Picchu are made of white granite, an igneous plutonic rock composed of quartz (60%), feldspar, and mica. This rock is easy to be worked or carved since it is not very hard if we want to compare it with the stone blocks of Q'oricancha in Cusco, Ollantaytambo in the Sacred Valley.

For the extraction of the stone blocks, the Incas must have used chisels made of bronze, an alloy of copper and tin, being in the category of *Mosh's scale* between 3 and 4, which is not a very hard metal if compared to steel. The workers of the Tawantinsuyo used different sizes of bronze chisels to make the holes, using at the same time stone hammers, making holes, and at a distance of one hand. Then, another hole was made, to introduce in these holes tree stakes, to pour water into them. These stakes swelled and helped to fragment the rock. This was one of the techniques used to fracture the rocks. However, in some cases, the fire must also have been used. The rock was heated and after a while, when it was very hot, water was poured on it. The sudden temperature change caused the fragmentation of the rock.

Machu Picchu. The *Inca Quarry*, geological chaos.

CHAPTER IX: MACHU PICCHU, INCA CITY

The Incas must have known different techniques to work the stone, for which they used the knowledge of the stonecutters of the Altiplano area, since in the city of Machu Picchu and the Ollantaytambo complex, the stepped sign, a representation of the Tiahuanaco culture, can be observed.

To transport the blocks, the Incas must have used a system of ramps. To move them from one place to another, they must have used tree trunks, round stones carved as rollers or boulders (river stones), being pulled by ropes, made of straw or llama skin leather, using at the time of transport, human strength, i.e. hundreds of people in front and behind the block. During this operation, the block was being carved and worked, to then be placed. At this moment, the last finishing touches were made. Once the stone masonry was placed, it was polished and given the final finish. In Machu Picchu, we find several enclosures that show these examples of how the stone blocks were worked, such as in the Temple of the Three Windows, or in the Main Temple.

Machu Picchu. Sample of how the Incas extracted the stone blocks from the quarries

After the quarry, we will visit an Inca plaza where there are two very important constructions: the Main Temple and the Temple of the Three Windows.

The Temple of the Three Windows

It is a construction of rectangular form, of three walls having in the part of the front in the middle, a pillar that must have served to sustain the roof. In this enclosure, in the back wall, there are three trapezoidal windows. They are oriented towards the San Gabriel mountain.

On June 21st, at the time of the winter solstice, the sun illuminates the entire building. The first rays go through the three windows, creating each one inside at the floor level of very bright

Machu Picchu and the *Temple of the Three Windows*. The projections of the sun's rays at the winter solstice.

CHAPTER IX: MACHU PICCHU, INCA CITY

rectangular-shaped rays. It is very similar to the phenomenon that occurs in the Temple of the Sun.

In the front of this enclosure, where the pillar is, there is a block of carved stone that has the shape of a chakana, or Andean cross, but in the middle, it means that the chakana would have been cut. This can be observed very clearly.

After illuminating the three windows, the sun will illuminate this block of stone, projecting to the west side, at floor level, in the shadow, creating the other half of the Andean cross. Stone and shadow will form the famous chakana, the same that was a representation of the culture of the Altiplano, or Tiawanaco. This would perhaps demonstrate that they could have been the masters in the stonework in the process of construction of the city of Machu Picchu, with the labor of the inhabitants of the Cusco valley and the people conquered by Pachacuteq. This representation is also found in the Ollantaytambo complex in the *Baños de la Ñusta* sector.

The type of architecture of this temple is an imperial Inca architecture, with carved stone blocks, joined without mortar or mud mortar.

On the left side of the temple, near the *Main Temple*, several stone blocks were in the process of being worked. They would be evidence that this enclosure was in the process of construction, and could demonstrate that Machu Picchu was not finished.

Here we also have a question: How many people were needed to build the Inca citadel? According to the studies made by local archaeologists, they indicate that possibly more than 40,000 or 50,000 people were needed, the same people who had to do it under the "labor tax" in the service of the State, labor for two to three months per year.

The Main Temple

As the Temple of the Three Windows, it is a rectangular construction with three open walls, but its architecture is finer, with blocks of carved and polished stones, joined one to another without the use of any mud mortar. In the upper part, there are several trapezoidal niches, where the ceremonial paraphernalia must have been placed. In the middle part, we find a large block that must have been used as the main altar.

Towards the right side, near the corner, you can see that this wall is collapsing. It must be understood that the city was built on top of a mountain, at an intermediate point between the Machu Picchu mountain and the Huayna Picchu mountain. At ground level, there are many hollows, or empty spaces, which in the rainy season will produce landslides, causing the collapse of the walls.

Machu Picchu and the *main temple*. In the right corner of this enclosure, you can see the collapse of the construction.

Likewise, for the construction of Machu Picchu, the Incas had to start building from the valley floor to the top utilizing the system of terraces, which protected and gave stability to the site.

This temple, by the type of very fine architecture, we would call it the *Temple of the Apu Machu Picchu*, because all this construction is oriented towards this mountain since from this point descends the water that supplies the Inca city.

The Intiwatana

Intiwatana, from *inti*, the sun, and *watana*, to tie up, or to tie, would mean, the "place where the sun is tied up or tied", and is located at the top of Machu Picchu. It is a rock carved and polished in situ, having the shape of a rhombus with four corners. Each corner is oriented to a cardinal point and each cardinal point is oriented to a mountain: to the north, the Huayna Picchu mountain, to the south; the Machu Picchu and in the distance, from the top of the Huayna Picchu mountain, you can see the apu Salkantay, to the west, the apu Pumasillo, and finally, to the east, the apu Veronica.

The Intiwatana has in the upper middle part, a pillar that must have served for the observation of the sun and the projections of shadows to determine the times of the year.

Nowadays, in the Peruvian Andes, especially in places where the main economy is agriculture, the farmer pays much attention to the behavior of the sun: At what time of the year is it, where does the sunrise occur? Indeed, the sunrise point varies during the year. They pay close attention to the flora, when certain species such as orchids or begonias bloom, as well as the fauna, when butterflies, wild birds such as hummingbirds, parrots, and other birds appear, to determine when to sow and harvest their agricultural fields.

Machu Picchu. The *Intiwatana* sector. The highest point in the Inca citade.

The Inca calendar begins in August when the Pachamama is celebrated. This makes more sense in the Andean world because we are at the beginning of the rainy season and planting season of agricultural products such as corn and potatoes, especially in those places where it is grown once a year, being very different in the valleys where it is grown twice a year, where there are rivers or streams. The water element is fundamental. A clear example is in the Sacred Valley, one hour from the city of Cusco.

On the side facing Inti Punku, the Intiwatana has an altar carved in situ, which must have been used to place offerings or as an observation point during the summer solstice.

Nearby, at ground level, there is an altar carved into the rock in a triangular shape, oriented towards the cardinal point south, that is, towards the city of Machu Picchu. Here there are many altars of different sizes, oriented not only to the sacred mountains but also to other mountains, giving Machu Picchu the sense of a sacred ceremonial center.

The highlight of the Intiwatana is that it is an intact construction, which indicates that the city was not discovered by the Spanish invaders during the colonial period that lasted almost 300 years. Although we have the information of the chronicles of the 16th and 17th centuries of the existence of the sector of "Piccho". This information of the chronicles refers to the geographical area that is those of the area of Piccho that had to pay the coca to the Spanish merchant, cabuya, or Andean maguey, chili, or fruit, such as pacae, avocado, ojotas, or shoes, made of cabuya and not properly to the city of Machu Picchu.

Machu Picchu. The *Intiwatana*, also known as "sundial".

The Main Square

This square is located in the middle part of the city, dividing it into two sectors: the religious sector and the urban sector. As in the large llaqtas, when the Incas built their plazas, they placed sand from the sea, sand from the rivers and seashells at floor level, representing Mama Cocha, from *mama*, or mother, and *cocha*, the sea, the lake, or the lagoon, representing the element of water.

The capital of the empire, Cusco, is located in the central part of the Andes. It was built, on its floor, with sand from the sea and seashells, which must have been brought from the Peruvian sea. For Machu Picchu, the floor of its main plaza must have been

Machu Picchu. The *main square* of the Sacred Llaqta.

made with sand brought from the floor of the Urubamba River valley.

The plaza of Machu Picchu must have been used for religious ceremonies or daily acts, but not for commercial activity, since in Inca times, the exchange of products took place on the outskirts of the cities, on the corners where the inhabitants could exchange corn, potatoes, coca leaves, and other products.

In Inca times, not only agricultural products were exchanged, but also construction materials: tree sticks, straw, ropes made of straw or llama hides, etc. On both sides of the plaza, there are cultivation terraces that must have been used to support the constructions, as well as for the cultivation of some varieties of plants.

The Sacred Rock

This is a carved rock that is located very close to the entrance to the Huayna Picchu mountain. According to the local guides, it would be the representation of the apu Yanantin, the mountain that is behind the rock, whose location is at the other end of the Urubamba River. But if you take a good look at it, it does not have the shape of the mountain.

Because of its shape, like the North American explorer Johan Reinhard, we support the idea that it must represent the apu Pumasillo, which is located at the west end of the Inca city. This rock was decorated in its surroundings by a wall that must have served as an altar for the placement of offerings, which are still made today.

In Inca times, when the inhabitants could not be so close to their tutelary gods, they carved the rock with the shape or silhouette of these apus to be worshipped.

Machu Picchu and the *Sacred Rock*. This formation has the shape of the apu Pumasillo, which is located at the west end of the Inca city.

During the colonial period, this tradition was replaced by images of saints or virgins with different names, a clear example being the San Gabriel mountain near the Inca city. Why San Gabriel? Because it has the shape of an angel with open wings. Perhaps that is the reason for the name of this mountain. It is also the case of the Veronica mountain. Because of its shape, it was given this name.

The Huayna Picchu mountain

This mountain is located at the northern end of the citadel. Its summit is 2,745 meters/9,004 feet high. If we compare with the general floor level of Machu Picchu, which is at 2,400 meters/7,872 feet, there would be a height difference of about 345 meters/1,132 feet in height.

CHAPTER IX: MACHU PICCHU, INCA CITY

In the Huayna Picchu, towards the left side, you have in the middle part, the road that leads to the summit: one hour of walking, only ascent. This road is very steep but paved with stone steps. From the top, you can see Machu Picchu in its entirety. Also, to the south side, there is an altar that must have served to place offerings or as an observation point for the winter and summer solstices.

Very close to the top, there is a dwelling that must have been used as a deposit to store some ceremonial utensils; and around it, there are many platforms that must have served as support or decorative platforms.

Machu Picchu. The Huayna Picchu mountain is located north of the sacred city

In the lower part, behind the mountain, there is another temple called the *Temple of the Moon*, which must have been a very important construction of ceremonial use associated with several enclosures. Little known and visited, it is a very interesting sector.

The urban sector

This sector is located between the Huayna Picchu mountain and the Temple of the Condor, on the left bank of the Urubamba River. It covers a large geographical area.

The urban sector is also named the *residential sector*, because of the type of construction, with a finer architecture, better distribution of the houses that are framed in the Inca style, and four rectangular-shaped enclosures around a central courtyard. Many of the buildings are built with carved stone masonry, joined with mud mortar and some of the enclosures must have fulfilled a very

Machu Picchu. The Urban sector. Shadow projections during the winter solstice.

important function. They are built with carved and polished stone masonry, but no mud mortar was used to join them together.

The urban or residential sector is made up of different groups of buildings, which were named after the studies conducted by Hiram Bingham, for a better understanding of how the Inca city was at the time of Tawantinsuyo. But all these constructions would require a change of names, more respectful with the historical and archaeological reality of Machu Picchu.

The city of Cusco, before the arrival of the Spaniards, had the shape of a puma, a sacred animal in Inca times. Its main square was the heart of puma city. Around it, the Incas built their main temples and the houses or palaces of the rulers.

In this sense, the ceremonial or religious sector would be located between the Temple of the Sun and the sector called the Sacred Rock; and the urban or residential part would be located between this Sacred Rock and the Temple of the Condor. This group would have small subsectors.

The Three Gates subsector

So-called because to enter this housing area, three access doors lead to different groups of enclosures, around the main courtyard. According to the studies carried out, this would be the sector where the chosen women were located, who were brought from different parts of the Inca Empire to do the work of weaving and making chicha, a drink used for religious ceremonies.

Also, this sector must have been inhabited by the families of the nobility of blood, belonging to the Inca, or the families of privilege, that is, the families of the chiefs or rulers of the conquered peoples, faithful to the Inca, who must have been occupied during the time in which the rulers performed their religious ceremonies. Once the ceremonies were over, these families had to return to their cities or towns where they lived permanently.

And these houses, in the absence of these families, must have been taken care of by the chosen women or by other similar people who performed domestic tasks.

Within this sector, there is also another subsector called *Casa de los Morteros* (The House of Morters).

The House of Morters

In this enclosure, in the interior, in the middle part at floor level, there are two mortars carved in stone of circular shape, which must have fulfilled a function of astronomical observation, that

Machu Picchu and the *House of the Mortars*. At ground level, there are water mirrors.

CHAPTER IX: MACHU PICCHU, INCA CITY

is to say, as water mirrors. These were filled with rainwater on nights with clear skies, without the presence of clouds. It was possible to observe, in these mirrors, the stars or the constellations of the Southern Hemisphere. These observations were used to organize the agricultural calendar that began in October, the season for sowing corn and potato seeds, as well as other agricultural products.

The Temple of the Condor

This temple is located at the end of the tour in the Inca citadel. This construction is formed by a rock carved in the shape of a

Machu Picchu. The *Temple of the Condor*. At floor level, the body and head of this sacred bird are carved in the rock.

condor with open wings, a sacred animal in Inca times, as well as the constructions that are in the upper part. It has behind this rock, towards the left side, some small trapezoidal niches that Hiram Bingham called the *sector of the jails*, to place in them the people that had broken or transgressed the rules of the State, but that rather, they should have served to place the important mummies and next to them to place certain offerings.

In the lower part, at floor level, in the 1990s, archaeologist Alfredo Valencia, in his archaeological excavations, found remains of Inca-style ceramic fragments, along with the skeletal remains of llamas. It is suggested that in Inca times, the sacrifice of black llamas was very common in religious ceremonies. The part of the condor's body would be the rock-carved at floor level that must have been used to make the sacrifices.

Why this Temple of the Condor in Machu Picchu? And why are there no other similar temples in the city of Cusco or the Sacred Valley? Because perhaps in the city of Machu Picchu, sometimes you are lucky enough to see this sacred bird flying overhead, and to capture its sacredness, the Incas built a temple dedicated to it.-

CHAPTER X
BASIC INFORMATION FOR THE TRAIL TO MAKE THE INCA TRAIL TO MACHU PICCHU

How is the Inca Trail program of 4 days and 3 nights?

The 4 days and 3 nights program are as follows:

Day 1: Cusco - Ollantaytambo - Piscacucho (Km. 82) - Huayllabamba

- Early morning pick up from the hotel at 5.00 a.m.
- Transfer to km 82/Piscacucho, by private transport (starting point of the trek), at 2,720 meters/8,922 feet above sea level.
- We start walking along the famous Inca trail, and we will see: Piscacucho, Qanabamba, Llaqtapata, and Willka Raqay.
- Lunch in the village of Tarayoc.
- Camping at Huayllabamba, 3,000 meters /9,840 feet above sea level.
- Walking distance: 13 km.

Day 2: Huayllabamba - Dead Woman's Pass - Pacaymayu

5:30 am: wake up time and breakfast.

THE INCA TRAIL TO MACHU PICCHU

- Surviving the highest pass on the way to Machu Picchu (Dead Woman's Pass): 4,215 meters/113,825 feet a.s.l., with incredible views and different ecosystems, flora, and fauna that change according to the altitude.
- Camping in the Pacaymayu valley at 3,600 meters/11,808 feet above sea level.
- Walking distance: 12 km.

Day 3: Pacaymayu - Runkuraqay - Sayacmarka - Phuyupatamarka - Intipata - Wiñaywayna
- Early wake-up and breakfast time.
- We will visit several archaeological sites: Runkuraqay, Sayacmarka, Phuyupatamarka, Intipata and Winaywayna.
- Camping at Wiñaywayna at 2,700 meters/8,856 feet asl.
- Walking distance: 16km

Day 4: Wiñaywayna - Sun Gate - Machu Picchu - Aguas Calientes Village - Cusco
- 3:30 am: Wake up time and breakfast.
- 5:00 am: Begin trek to Sungate (Intipunku).
- Guided tour in the city of Machu Picchu (optional: climb the Huayna Picchu mountain or Machu Picchu mountain according to availability).
- Bus to Aguas Calientes Pueblo for lunch.
- Train back to Ollantaytambo from Aguas Calientes.
- Bus to Cusco city from Ollantaytambo (leaving you at your hotel or accommodation).
- Walking distance: 6 km.
- End of the walk

How is the Inca Trail program of 2 days and 1 night?

The program of the Inca Trail of 2 days and 1 night is as follows:

Day 1: Cusco - Ollantaytambo - Km. 104 - Chachabamba - Wiñaywayna - Inti Punku - Machu Picchu - Aguas Calientes Pueblo (over nigth).

From the city of Cusco to the town of Ollantaytambo (train station). Then, we have two options:
- Option 1 - From Cusco to Ollantaytambo by car,
- Option 2 - One day before doing the two-day Inca Trail, the tourist can do the tour of the Sacred Valley (full day) and spend the night in Ollantaytambo and thus will not have to return to the city of Cusco. He/she will be able to rest and the next day of the trek, not getting up too early. This option is the most recommended.

Day 2: Aguas Calientes Pueblo - Machu Picchu city (optional Huayna Picchu and/or Temple of the Moon) - Aguas Calientes - Ollantaytambo - Cusco .

How to book the Inca Trail 4 days and 3 nights?

The Inca Trail to Machu Picchu (classic) is regulated by the Peruvian Government through the Ministry of Culture of Cusco. To do it we suggest the following recommendation:

Decide as soon as possible the exact date when you want to do the Inca Trail. Why? Because this trail has a maximum limit of people between tourists and support staff: 500 people per day (200 tourists and 300 support staff, which are local guides and porters. For this reason, you have to make the reservation many months in advance, especially in the high season of tourism in the city of Cusco: from May to September, for most tourists, summer vacation.

If you want to do the trail this season, we recommend you to book your place six or seven months in advance. For example, if the tourist would like to do the Inca Trail from May to October. We suggest you make your reservation in October or November of the previous year, to get the availability of spaces.

What does the tourist need to book the Inca Trail to Machu Picchu?

You need to send a "copy of your original passport", the same that you will use when you arrive in Cusco, either for your accommodation, purchase of train and bus tickets. This can be sent via the *Internet* or *Whatsapp* application.

If the tourist changes his "passport", he must bring both passports (old and new), which is an indispensable requirement for the purchase of tickets for the Inca Trail. In case your government, at the time of the change of passport, retains the old document, you must make a *color photocopy*. This will be presented at the time of the trek, showing both documents.

If the tourist is a student, send *a copy of his/her* university *student card*. This must be valid and will be shown at the beginning of the hike.

How to book if the tourist wants to do the "short Inca trail" (2 days and 1 night) to Machu Picchu?

The "short Inca trail" to Machu Picchu has greater availability of spaces, being able to make your reservation up to a month in advance. But if the tourist can do it with more time, it would be much better, especially for May to September.

CHAPTER X: BASIC INFORMATION

For this trek, it is not necessary to have the support staff (porters), who are the logistic staff, in charge of carrying the camping equipment. The tourist will only carry a small backpack carrying only the necessary things, because the hike is only one day, which takes 13 kilometers away, sleeping the first night in the town of Aguas Calientes or Machu Picchu Pueblo.

For which, it is also necessary to send copies of the original passport and student card if applicable. These will be shown at the beginning of the walk.

What equipment is needed for the 4 days and 3 nights Inca Trail?

If you decide to do the Inca Trail (classic), you need the following equipment:

1. Good hiking shoes (trekking boots), the brand you like, which should be very comfortable. Recommendation: Especially for beginner tourists. If they want to buy new shoes, they should be "one size too big". Why? Because feet swell when walking, and they need a little more space in the shoes. Because if you buy the exact size, after half an hour or an hour of walking, they will cause the famous blisters on your feet, especially when the trail is downhill, scraping your toes with the shoes.
2. A good, comfortable backpack of 20 or 30 liters, thinking that you will carry in it your personal belongings such as a water bottle, sunglasses, sunblock, mosquito repellent, snacks or energy bars, a thermal jacket, rain poncho, gloves, hat, cap, and camera (iPhone or cell phone), to take pictures or record videos and flashlight (headlight).
3. A good and comfortable sleeping bag, thinking that it will be used for three nights. Sleeping well makes the body rest

THE INCA TRAIL TO MACHU PICCHU

well and the next day when waking up, the tourist will feel with all the energy to continue with the adventure. On the Inca Trail, the second night (at the Pacaymayu camp), it is quite cold, reaching minus 05 degrees Celsius in the dry season.

4. A good sleeping mat (inflatable mattress), which is highly recommended. Most of the local travel companies provide a very simple sleeping pad, which is not very comfortable since the pad will be used for three nights and you will be sleeping on the floor.

5. A pair of trekking poles, as the Inca Trail is not a flat trek. It is uphill and downhill, and in the rainy season, in some places, the trail is very slippery. So, it is better to put it this way "it is easier to walk on four feet than on two feet or to walk on four legs than on two legs", especially if the tourist has knee and ankle problems.

6. Regarding the clothes to wear for four days, we recommend bringing: one or two trekking pants, a sweatshirt for the camps, a jacket for the cold, a rain jacket, three pairs of socks minimum, three pairs of underwear, three or four polo shirts, a pair of gloves, a scarf, a pair of sandals or a pair of light sneakers, a small towel, a book if you want to read, casinos if you want to play.

Here is a list to take for the Inca Trail, recommended by most travel agencies to their tourists :

- Original passport,
- Original student ID card, in case you are a student,
- Trekking boots,
- Backpack,
- Sleeping bag,

CHAPTER X: BASIC INFORMATION

- Mattress,
- Trekking poles,
- Warm clothing, especially for the nights (camps 1 & 2),
- Gloves,
- Flashlight (extra batteries especially for the last camp and the last day),
- Camera and cell phones (we recommend bringing a battery charger),
- Water bottle,
- Sunscreen,
- Sunglasses,
- Sun hat and wool cap (camp 2),
- Scarf and handkerchief,
- Rain jacket,
- Rain poncho (weather is very variable),
- Toilet paper,
- Small towel,
- "Snacks" and energy bars (chocolate, snickers or others),
- Personal medical prescription (your medications) if you have any allergies,
- Sandals and tennis shoes (light equipment to wear in the camps),
- Extra money (cash) for tips (in dollars and Peruvian currency).

What are the most common questions for the Inca Trail?

The questions most frequently asked by tourists about the famous Inca Trail to Machu Picchu, especially the 4-day, 3-night trek are:

1. What is the Inca Trail to Machu Picchu?

The Inca Trail is the network of roads that left from different places or villages, whose final destination was the sacred city of Machu Picchu. Today, the road to Machu Picchu is the best known of the South American countries and has as its starting point kilometer 82 or the area known as Piscacucho.

It was the Qapaqñan, the Inca road system that existed throughout the Tawantinsuyo territory until before the arrival of the Spaniards. These roads linked cities, villages, and valleys with different ecological levels, which can still be seen today in the Andean countries of the Southern Cone -Peru, Bolivia, Argentina, Chile, Ecuador, and Colombia-, as a millenary work.

The famous Inca trail to Machu Picchu, which is walked today, was one of the eight roads that led to this mythical city. Along the way, you can observe and visit Inca villages, resting places, warehouses, ceremonial sites, water sources, agricultural complexes and enjoy unique biodiversity.

2. Is it necessary to reserve the Inca Trail in advance?

Yes, it is necessary to book well in advance for the Inca Trail to Machu Picchu, because according to Peruvian government regulations, only 500 people (200 tourists and 300 local staff, who are support personnel, guides, cooks, and porters) per day can do this trek.

It is therefore essential to make your reservation many months in advance, especially in the high season (May to October), which in Cusco is the dry season, being this time for the northern hemisphere, spring, and summer. We recommend making your reservation six to seven months in advance, to get available.

For the Short Inca Trail, you can make your reservation only one or two months in advance, which is recommended, so that your guide or local travel agent can arrange hotel and train reservations.

CHAPTER X: BASIC INFORMATION

3. How many days does the Inca Trail to Machu Picchu take?

The Inca Trail to Machu Picchu has several options. The classic one takes four days and three nights, this is the program that most of the local tour companies offer on their websites, having for this trek already campsites designated by the Peruvian government, which offer the necessary facilities to the tourist.

But if you want to enjoy a better adventure, as a mountain guide, with more than 775 treks, I would recommend you to do the five days and four nights trek, to enjoy in a better way, camping in different places, far from the noise of the groups making the traditional trek.

There is another option, for the tourist who was not lucky enough to make a reservation for the traditional trail, but who wants to reach the city of Machu Picchu by foot, is the short trail of two days and one night. You can book it up to a month in advance since there is an availability of 200 people per day.

4. Is the Inca Trail a very difficult and dangerous hike?

This trail is a moderate hike, of flat places, of ascents and descents with large, regular, and small gradients, where the route must walk the use of trekking poles, especially in the rainy season, from December to May.

The trail is not dangerous if the hiker follows the rules and instructions of the mountain guides. You will be able to enjoy the best adventure, but it is always necessary to take precautions to avoid possible accidents.

THE INCA TRAIL TO MACHU PICCHU

5. Do I need to prepare myself physically for the Inca Trail?

If you want to make the trek to Machu Picchu, we recommend you to prepare yourself physically, because altitude sickness, or *soroche*, is the problem you have usually in the mountains, which causes some tourists to return to Cusco on the second day.

If you want to prepare yourself physically, we recommend you to do uphill and downhill trails, since the area to be covered, the terrain is very varied.

A very important recommendation is, for example, when you go to work, do not take the elevator. Take this route up the stairs to your place of work, the same when you return home. This exercise will help strengthen your legs, knees, and ankles and the days you decide to run. Another tip would be to carry a 20-liter backpack which will help your back and shoulders get stronger as well.

6. Could you give me altitude sickness?

The city of Cusco is located at an altitude of 3,400 meters/11,458 feet above sea level and the trailhead is 2,850 meters/9,605 feet above sea level. The highest level is 4,215 meters/13,825 feet asl and the lowest is 2,000 meters/6,560 feet asl.

Having a variety of altitudes, the first problem for the tourist who comes to visit Cusco and do the Inca Trail, is the soroche. For this, we recommend spending two to three days in Cusco to acclimatize. The first day would be to rest in your lodging, but if you do not have any discomfort, we suggest you visit the city and the second day to explore the Sacred Valley or surrounding places, so you can get used to it.

And at the same time, the first days before the trek, for breakfast, lunch, and dinner, have a light diet, because the meals in the city of Cusco are heavy. Usually, the people of Cusco, after lunch

CHAPTER X: BASIC INFORMATION

and dinner, drink a hot mate (mate de muña, yerba buena, anise, or chamomile), or take a small glass of liquor or pisco, which helps the digestion of the stomach.

7. When is the best time of the year to travel the Inca Trail?

The city of Cusco has two climatic seasons: the rainy season (October to May) and the dry season (June to September). In Cusco, the climate is very different than in the northern hemisphere, the temperatures are very changeable.

The best time to do the Inca Trail would be in the dry season. However, keep in mind that in most countries in the northern hemisphere, it is spring and summer season. In the city of Cusco, it is the high season, the time when most tourists decide to do this famous trail. Therefore it is advisable to make your reservations in advance. The rainy season is also a good time to do this tour, as you can enjoy the local flora and fauna. The interesting thing is that in Cusco, there is no constant rain. It can rain for half an hour or a couple of hours, so it is advisable to have a poncho or a waterproof jacket to help you enjoy this adventure.

8. Can children do the Inca Trail?

Children, if they can do the Inca Trail to Machu Picchu, many of them have enough energy to walk, they are curious and ask many questions. But like all children full of curiosity, many times they do not measure the accidents that could happen along the hike, so it is advisable to walk with parents or walk with the mountain guide. In my years of experience, I have had in my groups, children as young as five years old, and in my personal experience, it is the children who make the adventure happy.

9. Am I worried that I might be too slow to walk?

Generally, all groups are mixed, of different nationalities, ages, cultures, and physical states. The Inca Trail is a hike, not a marathon or race. The idea is to enjoy this hike. Passengers should walk at their own pace, without the necessary hurry, for this, the travel agencies have the services of local guides, who are knowledgeable about this route and will provide all the facilities, such as services, times, and the necessary help that the tourist needs.

10. What happens if I get sick and need to come back?

According to the regulations of the Inca Trail, when the groups are less than nine people, a mountain guide is in charge of the group. When the groups are more than this number, two guides are in charge of the group.

When a person feels very bad, generally there are two, the most frequent cases: altitude sickness or stomach problems, depending on the physical condition of the tourist. It is the main guide who organizes the necessary facilities for the tourist to return to the city of Cusco or continue the hike to Machu Picchu. The good thing about the Inca Trail is that on day 1 or day 2 you can count on some facilities such as horse transportation and the help of some of the porters to return to the starting point or the end of this trek, the Inca city of Machu Picchu.

11. What do we do with the water on the walk?

On the Inca Trail, day 1 from the starting point to the first camp, along the way, there are several places where tourists can buy bottles of water, soft drinks, or snacks. On the second day, from the first camp to the place called Llulluchapampa, there are also two places where you can stock up on water and light food. But from Llulluchapampa, the travel agencies provide cold boiled water to fill the bottles, where it is no longer necessary to use purifying tablets.

From the starting point to the citadel, there is a water service in different places, especially in the official campsites. If the tourist wants to fill his bottle individually, it will be necessary to use purifying tablets, filter, to avoid stomach problems.

12. Who are the porters?

The porters are local people from the Sacred Valley, as well as from different parts of the city of Cusco. They are the people in charge of carrying the trekking equipment such as personal tents, dining tents, kitchen tents, food, and other materials necessary for the trek.

According to the use of the Inca Trail, arranged by the Peruvian government, each porter can only carry 20 kilos, plus his personal equipment (sleeping bag, sleeping mat, and clean clothes). As a general rule, each porter carries approximately 25 to 26 kilos.

13. Once I booked, can I change my departure date?

Once you have made your reservation for the Inca Trail, it is *no* longer *possible to* change the date. This is following the regulations set forth by the central government.

Besides, the Peruvian government does not reimburse or return the money, so it is recommended to make this reservation, having already thought about the exact date to make, to avoid unnecessary problems.

14. Where do I keep my bags while I am doing the Inca Trail?

In the city of Cusco, all large or small accommodations, from 5-star hotels to hostels, offer as part of the service, the "Storage" service, where tourists can store their personal belongings (suitcases, backpacks, etc.), until the time of their return to the city of Cusco or the Sacred Valley.

15. Are there any bathrooms on the Inca Trail?

On the Inca Trail throughout the route, lunch places, and official campsites, there are bathrooms, which are very basic services, where it is necessary to carry toilet paper. Some local travel agencies offer as part of the service bathroom tents with a small latrine.

On the first day of the trek, local families offer bathing services (real baths). Then, the tourist will have to pay one sol for the use of this service.

16. What is the food like, should I bring food?

All travel agencies include in their service the necessary food, which is very varied and balanced. They offer three breakfasts, three lunches, and three dinners.

Most travel agencies do not include these services on the first day (breakfast) and the last day (lunch).

If any tourist has problems with allergies or is vegetarian, he/she should indicate this at the time of booking and should remind the mountain guide, on the first day, before starting the trek so that the cook can buy some more suitable food.

It is worth remembering that Peruvian cuisine is one of the best cuisines in the world.

17. Can I do the Inca Trail alone or on my own?

The Inca Trail to Machu Picchu is regulated by the Peruvian government, so it is not possible to do it on your own. Tourists must hire the services of a travel agency and be accompanied by guides who are authorized by the Regional Directorate of Culture of Cusco (DDC-Cusco) and SERNANP. Likewise, travel agencies must be authorized by the government.

CHAPTER X: BASIC INFORMATION

The groups can be small, less than eight people, with a maximum number of tourists in the group of sixteen people, for which there will be a guide or two professional tour guides with the respective authorization.

18. Can anyone do the Inca Trail hike?

The Inca Trail is a great adventure that generally takes four days and three nights. All people who have the energy to do this great adventure are invited to make this trek, from children to seniors, but who have the physical conditions to be able to walk in the mountains, for which they must prepare themselves adequately in their place of origin.

19. What is prohibited during the Inca Trail?

The Inca Trail is regulated by the Ministry of Culture of Cusco (DDC-Cusco) and SERNANP, institutions that are responsible for ensuring its protection, care, and use. Tourists must respect and abide by the rules of the trail, such as no campfires in the campsites, no climbing on the Inca walls, no littering on the trail, no destruction of the local flora and fauna.

You will have to follow all the rules that your mountain guide will indicate to you, for better enjoyment of this great adventure.

20. Is it possible to charge the batteries of cell phones or other devices in some camp ?

On the first day of the trek, upon arrival at the first campsite, tourists have the option of recharging the batteries of their cameras or cell phones. The following three days, until reaching Aguas Calientes, there is no such service. Therefore, it is advisable to carry a battery recharger or a solar recharger in your backpack.

21. How do we return to Cusco after visiting Machu Picchu?

After finishing the trek, most travel agencies offer as part of the service, the return train, which is the train from Aguas Calientes to Ollantaytambo; and then from there to the city of Cusco in a car or minibus.

We recommend, when making your reservation, to check with your travel agent which train you wish to return to the city of Cusco and its schedule.

22. Should we hire a porter for this tour?

All travel agencies offer the service of porters, who are in charge of carrying the trekking equipment and food. The porters are not in charge of carrying your personal belongings.

For better enjoyment, when making your reservation, we recommend that you secure the services of *an extra porter*, who will be the person who will carry your personal belongings throughout the Inca Trail.

Each agency offers a personal porter service, six to eight kilos, or more if necessary. This way, you will only be able to carry a small backpack with the things you need for the day.

23. Why should I trust a travel agency for the Inca Trail?

Travel agencies must have the proper authorization assigned by the DIRCETUR (Regional Tourism Directorate), the SERNANP (National Service of State Protected Areas), and the Ministry of Culture, to operate in the network of the road to Machu Picchu, which is regulated by the Peruvian government.

CHAPTER X: BASIC INFORMATION

24. How can I locate Hilbert Sumire for mountain guide services for the Inca Trail ?

Hilbert Sumire is very easy to locate!
His personal email address is: hilbertsumire@gmail.com
On Facebook, like Hilbert Sumire
Instagram, like hilbertperu
On YouTube, as HilbertPeru

Basic equipment for the Inca Trail.

THE INCA TRAIL TO MACHU PICCHU

CHAPTER XI
STORIES OF THE INCA TRAIL

As a Mountain Guide, in my 25 years of experience, a great number of stories have happened to me, sometimes unbelievable. I would like to share some of them with adventurous people.

Hold your llamas!

About eighteen years ago, when I was on one of my treks on the Inca Trail to Machu Picchu, I had a group of eighteen tourists of different nationalities. In the group, there was an American family made up of dad, mom, and a teenage son of about fifteen years old.

For me, the first day of trekking, is a test as a mountain guide, to verify how many people walk well, how many walk slowly, how many have a normal pace, how many walk fast. It is also a good test to know how many tourists have problems with soroche, which is very common in the mountains.

In those days, there were no rules of the road. The tour companies organized their groups according to the owners' criteria. There were two local guides, one guide who went in front of the group and the second one who went behind the last passenger.

Then, because of my years of experience as a lead guide, I would go after the last tourist. When the group was large, during the hike, I would always come and talk to the passengers and sometimes ask them if they had altitude sickness.

On the first day, after having walked about four hours, after lunch, on the way to the first camp called Huayllabamba, the last passenger of the group, an American citizen, was asking me every 20 or 25 minutes, how was the second day of the hike and if it was very difficult. This was because she wanted to return to Cusco on the first day. She was very scared about the second day of the trek. She thought she would not be able to do it. From time to time she asked me:

— Hilbert, do you think I can do it tomorrow?

— Yes, you can do it, I replied.

As a professional, I don't like to tell the tourist to go back to the city to avoid problems, although it might be the quickest solution. I was thinking at the time: coming to Peru from the United States is not easy. It is time and money. She planned this trip to Peru, wanting to make this trek to Machu Picchu is a dream. It is a challenge. There are too many things or ideas together to go back without going all the way. I told her:

— Today is the first day. We have an hour and a half hike to the first camp. The trail is smooth. If you would like, I could help you carry your backpack to lighten the weight.

— Thank you, Hilbert, she replied.

She was a little calmer after that. But then, again, she would ask me if she could do the second day's stretch and she was still thinking about going back to Cusco. So I answered her:

— Today is day one and not day two. If you want to return to Cusco, you could do it tomorrow.

On the second day, before breakfast, the passenger asked me one more time:

— How difficult is the walk?

I replied:

— We have six hours of climbing, but it will be at a very slow pace. I will be with you, every step of the way.

But she was so nervous, after asking me and asking me again, I told her:

— If you want to return to Cusco, you can do so. I have already arranged for a porter to carry your personal belongings. You will be accompanied by the second guide as well.

She answered me:

— Hilbert, I don't want to go back to Cusco. What happens is that I am afraid that I will get altitude sickness.

To which I replied:

— Let's decide now, but I have a couple of questions for you, and I would like you to answer me honestly... Do you have altitude sickness, headaches, vomiting, dizziness?

— No, she replied.

— Do you have stomach aches, nausea, allergies, asthma, or similar problems?

— No.

— Do you have physical problems, leg pain, ankle pain, knee pain, or some kind of problem that you don't want to tell me about? Please...

— No, no.

And I added:

— If you do not have altitude sickness, vomiting, dizziness; and if your stomach is fine, you have no physical problems... What is the problem?

She answered me:

— Hilbert, I am afraid.

— You have no problem. If you want to return to Cusco, you can do so. It is your decision, not mine. But if you want to do the Inca Trail, I will help you, and I will help you carry your backpack, and we will walk together.

She nodded. The rule was to walk uphill every five minutes to stop and take a short break, that she would forget about the group, because, in the group, several passengers walked very well.

I told the second guide to go ahead with the group. I would go with the passenger and her husband, who was accompanying us.

Before leaving the camp, I told her that during the hike, if she felt or had any problems to let me know immediately. She said: I would.

We had a six-hour hike. We left together. She was a little nervous, we walked for five minutes. I asked her:

— How are you doing?

— I'm fine, she replied

We had a five-minute break and continued on our way. We walked for half an hour, and when we got to the next break, the husband said to her:

— Come on woman, everyone is waiting for you.

Imagine walking for an hour, two hours, and every time we came to rest, the husband told his wife:

— Come on woman, everyone is waiting for you.

After three hours of walking, once again, the husband said to the wife:

— Come on woman, everyone is waiting for you.

She was already very enraged and answered him:

- Shut up! son of a bitch; take it easy, hold your horses.

I had understood the first part immediately, "son of a bitch". But I hadn't understood when she said: "take it easy, hold your horses". Later, I asked her what that expression meant. She answered me:

— If someone is rushing you to do some things and you can't do it at that moment, in the United States, Americans have this expression, "take it easy, hold your horses".

When she finished explaining, I just understood the message of that sentence and I thought it was very funny at the time.

CHAPTER XI: STORIES OF THE INCA TRAIL

For my next Inca Trail trip, I changed this expression to "take it easy, hold your llamas," because instead of *horses*, the animal that represents the Inca culture is the llama.

But let's continue. After seven or eight hours (I don't remember very well), we reached the highest point of the trail: the famous point called the "Dead Woman's Pass" or Warmiwañuska, at 4,215 meters/13,825 feet. Upon reaching the summit, the passenger cried tears of joy because she had conquered her fear and made her challenge a reality. It was an emotional moment of joy and hugs with her husband. I remember that the couple's son had not waited for the parents. I told them not to worry, if he didn't wait for us, he was probably already at the camp with the group.

We had a two-hour hike to camp. She was already feeling much better. In some places, the pace was quicker. When we arrived at the second camp, the whole group was waiting for us and when they saw us arriving all tired, they applauded us. This was a very comforting and great joy.

The following day, day three, the passenger and her husband had to leave the camp very early in the morning, accompanied by the second guide, to advance and, little by little, reach the last point. That day was also a great challenge for her, who also arrived very tired and exhausted.

On the fourth day, we left the last camp together, on the way to Inti Punku, or the Sun Gate. Many people passed us, looked at us and other people asked us if we were okay if we needed any kind of help. I remember that we were the last people to arrive at Inti Punku. But we arrived with joy. When we crossed the gate and saw the Inca city of Machu Picchu, it was a huge joy for the passenger and her husband.

Those efforts are what we have to do in our lives, as people, challenges that we think might be difficult but not impossible to achieve, with effort and a little help. Everything is possible. That is the memory I have of many, to see the joy and happiness of your passengers to reach Machu Picchu, walking, not giving up, having the will and energy to meet this challenge. Take it easy, hold your llamas!

A great challenge

As a mountain guide, it is normal to have a mixed group, passengers of different nationalities, different customs, cultures, and ages.

One day before the Inca Trail, the travel companies organize the "*briefing*", which is the orientation given to the tourist. The itinerary of the trip is explained to them, how many hours they will have to walk per day, what we will see on the trip, what to take as trekking equipment, and also to ask if any passenger has any kind of allergies in terms of food or health problems.

On one of my trips, in the group, there was a Belgian tourist, who was doing the trek alone and who was traveling in South America for several months. As a rule, on the Inca Trail when the group is a number 6, 8, 14, or an even number, two people share a tent. If the number of passengers is an odd number like 7, 11, 13, one person sleeps alone. Luckily this passenger slept alone and did not need to share the tent.

On the first day, everyone in the group arrived safely at the first camp. One of the adventure rules is that the main guide has to ask everyone in the group about their state of health if they are well if anyone has altitude sickness or stomach problems. At the end of dinner on the first day ask the group:

— How are you doing?

All the people responded to me that they were very well and that they had no problems or discomfort.

On the second day, before starting the hike, I asked them again if everyone was okay, to which they replied that they were fine and without any problems.

After having walked for three hours, on the way up towards the first pass of Warmiwañusca (Dead Woman's Pass), the Belgian passenger named Emilie had a very pale face, almost yellow. I asked her if she was okay, and she replied that her stomach was hurting and she felt like throwing up.

Hearing this, I told her to rest, if she wanted to vomit she should do it to vote out all the bad things in his stomach. I told her if he wanted to go to the bathroom, showing her where it was located. I also asked her if she had diarrhea.

CHAPTER XI: STORIES OF THE INCA TRAIL

She said yes, her stomach hurt and she wanted to use the bathroom. I told her to go and take her time. When the passenger came back from the bathroom, I asked her how she was feeling now. She replied:

— I feel very bad, my stomach hurts.

Then I asked her other questions. If she had any allergies to any medicines. She answered that no, she did not have any allergies. As she had diarrhea, I gave her some pills to control it.

— Drink some non-carbonated coke, it will help.

After taking the pills and the coke, she felt a little better. But after five minutes she ran to the bathroom again. After waiting for her, I asked her again:

— How do you feel?

— I feel very bad? She replied:

— Rest a little longer, I told her.

As mountain guides, we are always willing to help our tourists, but when circumstances are difficult, one has to make the decision.

— We have already been waiting and helping you for an hour. Sorry, you must return to Cusco city or go back to Ollantaytambo village.

Ollantaytambo is a small town on the route, in the direction of the starting point of the Inca Trail. And I continued:

— There is a medical post, the doctors will be able to help you better than I can. They will also be able to give you better care and the right medicine.

— Please don't, she said. I don't want to go back to Cusco. The Inca Trail is a personal challenge, I want to finish it.

She added:

— It is not easy to come to Peru, especially when you come from a country as far away as Belgium.

After looking at her for a couple of minutes. I said to her :

— Rest twenty more minutes and we will see what happens. If you are still sick, I will be sorry, you will have to go back to Cusco, you should not continue walking and straining if you are still having stomach pains and vomiting.

After ten minutes I asked her again:

— How are you, Emilie?

— Much better, she replied I asked:

— Will you be able to walk?

— Yes, but slowly...

After walking together for fifteen minutes, I saw that the second guide, Omar, was looking at us all the time, surprised and not knowing how to help us. Along this small stretch, many mountain guide friends looked at me and told me in Spanish that I should send her to Cusco with the second guide to avoid many problems. One less passenger in the group will not take away the enthusiasm of the group, plus the rest of the people would understand.

Whenever someone told me something or made a recommendation in Spanish, I think Emilie understood by the looks and gestures my friends made.

She said to me:

— Please, I do not want to return to Cusco.

As a mountain guide, my job is to help tourists make their dreams come true. I didn't give it much thought. I told Omar, the second guide:

— Help me with the passenger.

— How can I help you?

— Carry my backpack. I'll carry the passenger...on my back.

— Are you sure?

— Yes, I will.

Then I said to the passenger:

— The way to help you and keep you going is just by charging you.

She said to me:

— No, I can walk, but very slowly and I will rest for a couple of minutes.

So we started to move forward, but every time I stopped to rest, she rested for eight to ten minutes. I was worried because we would arrive very late at the camp. After talking to her and explaining the situation to her, we would be overtaken by night, and walking in the dark is dangerous because we could slip. She understood me.

CHAPTER XI: STORIES OF THE INCA TRAIL

— It doesn't matter if other tourists or porters look at us and comment. Don't pay attention to them.

I put it on my back and started carrying it. Carrying sixty kilos on my back, uphill was very hard. I think I carried it for twenty minutes. I never pretended to believe I was a superhero, but sometimes circumstances make you make decisions, good, bad or foolish.

At the time I thought charging it was a good idea, but after about ten minutes, I realized that it was very difficult.

— It is very difficult, I told her. We'll do it another way, we'll walk together, I'll help

She put one of her arms around my neck and I put my right arm around her waist to help her walk. I told her we would have to walk for five minutes and take a break for five minutes. We did that for twenty minutes. Then we had to change our pace. We walked for ten minutes and rested for five minutes, and so we continued walking, as the expression goes "slowly but surely".

Upon reaching the highest point of the trail, Dead Woman's Pass (4,215 meters/13,825 feet), the Belgian passenger felt much better and happy to have reached this summit. From time to time she took a sip of Coca-Cola without gas.

— We reached the highest point. Now I know I will be able to finish this challenge," she said, a little calmer.

We rested at the pass for a few minutes, as it was cold. We started to descend to the second camp called Pacaymayu, arriving before nightfall. Arriving at the camp, I told the cook to prepare for the passenger chicken soup for dinner. After taking her to her tent, she rested for half an hour. After that, she ate the chicken soup. She finished it very slowly, then rested in her sleeping bag.

The following day, the third day of trekking, is the longest stretch of the Inca Trail, as you have to walk 16 kilometers. She left very early from the second camp, accompanied by the second guide. I told the passenger:

— You will not have to carry anything, your personal belongings and water will be brought to you by the second guide.

She started walking very early, before the whole group and arriving to the lunch place, she was much better. I asked her how she was feeling. She replied that she was feeling much better and thanked me for not making her go back to Cusco.

After lunch, the passenger could already walk with the whole group, enjoying the hike, as well as the explanations of the Inca sites. When we showed her the Machu Picchu mountain, she felt very happy.

— There is only one day left to get to Machu Picchu.

On the fourth day of the trek, the passenger was feeling much better. She was able to carry her backpack with all her personal belongings. That morning, when we arrived at Machu Picchu she started to cry. She said:

— It was a personal challenge, to be able to finish the whole trek. The Inca Trail is a dream come true. My parents would be proud that I was able to finish the Inca Trail and that I didn't give up this challenge. They didn't think I could do it.

She added proudly:

— Challenge accomplished!

Hearing those words, I felt proud to have helped someone, and deep inside me, I thought that challenges are there to be met. Sometimes people need the help of other people to fulfill these dreams. In return she gave me a big kiss on the cheek, telling me:

— Thank you very much, Hilbert, for all your help.

Everyone in the group laughed, saying that a great girl from Belgium had won. I replied that I had won a great friend from Belgium and that I had also taken it as a challenge. Together we had made it happen. Together, united, we can make things easier. As the saying goes, *"today for you, tomorrow for me"*.

The biggest problem as a guide

As a mountain guide, in all my years of experience, the biggest problem I had, I think it was (I don't remember the year), ten or eleven years ago.

CHAPTER XI: STORIES OF THE INCA TRAIL

It was a mixed group, with passengers of different nationalities, consisting of sixteen people. In the group, there was a couple from Germany who were doing the Inca Trail with their best friend. I don't remember their names well.

On day two, as a rule of the Inca Trail, I came walking with the last person in the group. As a guide, the rule is simple, the passenger who is ahead of the group is fine, but, the passenger who walks behind, closing the group, is the passenger who might need my help.

When we arrived at the second camp, with the last person, I began to ask the members of the group how they were, how they were feeling, if anyone had headaches, altitude sickness or if anyone had stomach problems. This German passenger told me:

— I have a little headache and a little dizziness.

— Have you taken any medication?

— No, she replied.

— Do you have any allergies, I could give you some pills.

I had a first aid kit in my backpack, and I had some local pills for altitude sickness. She answered me:

— I don't want to take pills, she said. Will you have oxygen?

As part of the Inca Trail regulations, mountain guides are required to carry an oxygen

You must lie down in their tent, we will provide you with oxygen.

After lying down in his sleeping bag, we give her oxygen. After three to five minutes, and within ten minutes of giving her oxygen support, ask her :

— How do you feel? She replied:

— I feel much better now. For tomorrow I will need the help of a porter to carry my backpack.

— Don't worry, I will arrange for a porter to carry your backpack.

After that she went to sleep with her husband, saying goodbye. The next morning, very early, it would be 6.00 am. At the time of the "wake up with the mate de coca", the porters began to wake up the passengers. When I heard them, I also woke up and when I opened my tent and got up, I asked the passenger who was also coming out of her tent how she was feeling.

She turned around, looked at me, said:

— Better.

But from one moment to the next she fell to the ground, shaking her body as if she were having a seizure, convulsing her body, and vomiting. I never had this kind of problem before, as a mountain guide. The most common ones are altitude sickness, stomach pain, or ankle problems, but seeing the passenger convulsing scared me. It was the first time I had seen a female passenger have that kind of problem in the middle of the mountain.

The husband got out of the tent and picked up his wife. The best friend who had a tent nearby also got up and left the tent. So did the other passengers

In the desperation of the moment, as a guide, I shouted to the other groups camping in the same place, asking for the help of a doctor. In those brief minutes, everyone panicked, not knowing what was happening. Everyone wanted to help. At that moment, from a neighboring group, an English doctor came to help us. He looked at the passenger, started to ask her questions, but she did not answer anything. She kept shaking her body. The doctor told the husband to calm down, that we should move a little to give the passenger room to breathe.

After a few minutes, the passenger stopped shaking her body, but when the doctor asked her questions about her name and where she was. She did not answer anything, she had a look towards the sky. The doctor asks:

— Who is the main guide of the group?

— My name is Hilbert, I am the main guide.

— I organize a group of people to immediately evacuate the passenger.

I had to immediately call the leader of the carriers to organize a group of six men to load the passenger on a stretcher. The only way out was to go to Machu Picchu or to the town of Aguas Calientes, where there were doctors. At that point, we looked for help from everywhere. The park rangers came to

CHAPTER XI: STORIES OF THE INCA TRAIL

the camp and we asked them to help us with their stretcher and to provide us with a couple of people to help us carry the passenger.

Using the radios that the park rangers have, we called the city of Cusco to inform the travel agency of what was happening.

— We urgently need the services of a helicopter to evacuate a passenger. After waiting for a response, the travel agency office told us:

— There are no helicopters in the city of Cusco, they would have to send it from Lima.

Time was gaining on us. At that point, the doctor asked the passenger's husband if she had any health problems or allergies.

The husband replied:

— She had no allergies, didn't drink alcohol, didn't smoke. She was even a good diver.

It was a very tense time. We went all over the camp, asking all the guides to help us with their oxygen balloons. After giving help to the passenger, the English doctor told me:

— Hilbert, your passenger is in very bad shape. You need to evacuate her immediately and not waste any more time.

I didn't understand what was happening at that moment.

— What's wrong, doctor?

— She is very bad, and you have to immediately bring her down as low as possible.

Hearing this, I said to the second guide

— Alex, you are in charge of the group. If you need help with the organization of the group, the porter leader will help you with lunch, camp, and dinner.

Using the stretcher that the park rangers had, we carried the passenger. We had to tie her legs and body with straps so that when we loaded her, she would not fall. Without wasting much time, the porters began to load without taking many breaks. Even the cook of the group, Hilario, who was the

THE INCA TRAIL TO MACHU PICCHU

oldest cook in the company, upon seeing my concern, also helped us and accompanied us.

Up the stairs, walking fast, after carrying half an hour, I realized that one of the park rangers was taking a lot of pictures of us. I asked him:

— Why do you take pictures?

He answered me:

— It's for my photos, about how I work in the mountains.

— If you keep taking pictures, I'll break your camera. You are here to help us, a passenger's life is at risk.

From the second camp to Machu Picchu is 22 kilometers away, but the Inca trail in some parts is very narrow. There were moments of great tension. Seeing the husband crying for his wife, the friend who did not know what to do, and us hoping to get to Machu Picchu as quickly as possible.

When we arrived almost to the third pass of Phuyupatamarka, Dr. Oscar, who worked in the last camp (Wiñaywayna), caught up with us. At that time, in the last camp, there was a government construction that was managed by a private company providing restaurant services, bar, bathrooms, showers and as part of the service also provided the services of a doctor for passengers who were with some illness. Dr. Oscar asked me:

— What happened, what's wrong with the passenger?

— She was in very bad shape, unresponsive, unconscious.

The doctor, after checking her, told me:

— I think she has cerebral edema.

— Why what could have happened?

— Her brain was not well oxygenated. She was given some pills for altitude sickness or oxygen.

— She has not been given any pills, we were just giving her oxygen.

The doctor gave her, in a bottle, a mixture of water with coramine, which is a pill that has sugar in it. He made the passenger drink it. After giving her the aid, we continued carrying her. By that time we were alone, some of the

CHAPTER XI: STORIES OF THE INCA TRAIL

park rangers who were helping us had disappeared, only the porters, the cook, the passengers, and the doctor were left.

This time with the help of the doctor and the passengers we had to carry her. When we arrived at the last camp in Wiñaywayna, the doctor wanted to check her in his small office. When he saw her, the passenger had urinated in her pants. With the help of a camp worker, they changed her clothes.

In this camp, there is a cell phone signal. I had to call Cusco, the office of the travel agency, to coordinate the transportation of a train from Machu Picchu to Ollantaytambo and an ambulance from Ollantaytambo to the city of Cusco.

From the last camp to Machu Picchu is 6 kilometers. We did it in an hour and a half, with a lot of nervousness. Then, from Machu Picchu to the town of Aguas Calientes, we took a tourist bus. I remember that when we arrived in Aguas Calientes there was no train assistance. When I asked why there was no train I was told that I had to pay first.

I did not understand. I explained to her husband that we had to pay for the train transportation. He replied that, at that time, they did not have enough money.

The travel company had a hostel. The father of the owner of the company was the manager. When I explained to him the situation I was in, he lent me some money to pay for the transportation, but he did so very hesitantly, perhaps thinking that I would lose the money I borrowed. We took a small train, which is known as "el chismoso". It is a small train that goes in front of the tourist trains, to check if the route is ok, and to see if there are any problems.

When we arrived at the Ollantaytambo train station, an ambulance was waiting for us along with Dr. Tejada. Upon receiving the passenger, she was immediately put into the ambulance. The passenger's friend and I had to arrange another transport from Ollantaytambo to Cusco. Upon arrival in Cusco, we went directly to the clinic, which was a private clinic. After waiting for more than an hour, the doctor, a neurologist, told us that the passenger had had cerebral edema and that she was in care and would receive treatment.

The husband and the friend stayed at the clinic to see how the passenger was doing. After receiving the doctor's explanations I called the owner of the company to explain how the passenger was doing, what bothered me about the call was that the owner of the company kept me on hold for twenty minutes.

The next day, I took the company bus to Ollantaytambo and from there took the train to Machu Picchu. Arriving in Aguas Calientes, I went to the company's hostel, which was the place for lunch. At about 1.00 pm the passengers began to arrive. Each one began to ask me questions:

— How was the German passenger?

I would answer them:

— She is still unconscious and was in the care of doctors.

That night upon returning to the city of Cusco, the whole group decided to go to the company's office. The passengers wanted to talk to the owner. I went in to explain that the passengers wanted to talk to him. They wanted some way to help the passenger. He replied that everything was fine, that they did not need any help. As I left the office, I told the passengers that the owner of the company did not want to talk to them. They found this very strange.

The following day, in the evening hours, I went to the private clinic of Dr. Tejada, who took us to Ollantaytambo. The clinic was located very close to the Avenida del Sol, in the Grace passage. When I entered the passenger's room, she, who was lying on the bed, leaned back and called me:

— Hilbert, it is you, my guide.

When I heard my name I was happy. The husband said to her:

— Yes, it's Hilbert, relax, lie down on the bed, please.

The husband said to me:

— She needs to rest.

CHAPTER XI: STORIES OF THE INCA TRAIL

I left the room. At that moment the doctor was coming to check her. He asked me if I was his guide. I said yes.

The doctor told me:

— You did a good job, you evacuated this passenger. If she stayed any longer in the mountains, she would die. I don't know how you and your porters did it, but you helped save a life.

As I left the clinic. The passenger's husband said to me:

— Hilbert, thank you very much.

— I am happy that your wife has woken up and that she is going to get better. We all work together, porters, Hilario, you and your friend. I had never had anything like this happen to me in the mountains. This time I had learned a great life lesson. And I gave him a big hug.

A true story.

As a mountain guide, we are sometimes unprepared for this type of accident or incident in the mountains, we can only learn from each moment, a great life lesson.

Since that trip, I have learned a rule that I always use on my trips. To always ask the passengers how they feel, if they have problems with altitude sickness, dizziness, or stomach problems, and to carry in my backpack, a small oxygen balloon, which could make a big difference in the mountains.

The life of a person in the mountains often depends on how we act at that moment.

BIBLIOGRAPHY

AGURTO CALVO, Santiago, "Construcción, arquitectura y planeamientos Incas", Lima, 1987.

ALEGRIA SANCHEZ, Richard "Wiñaywayna: Causes of the instability of the Inca structure", (National Institute of Culture), 2001.

ANGLES VARGAS, Victor, "Historia del Cusco Incaico" (3 volumes), Lima, 1988, "Machu Picchu and the Inca Road / Y el Camino Inca", Lima, 2002.

AVENDAÑO FARFAN, Angel, Pachacuteq, Municipality of Qosqo, Cusco, 1992.

BARREDA MURILLO, Luis, "Historia y Arqueologia del Qosqo Pre - Inka", Revista, Instituto de Arqueologia Andina, Machu Picchu, 1995.

BETANZOS, Juan D., "Suma y Narración de los Incas", Madrid, 2004, 1551.

BINGHAM, Hiram, "Inca Land: Explorations in the Highlands of Peru", Boston, 1922, "Lost City of the Incas" Condor Book, Lima, 1997.

CABIESES, Fernando, "Machu Picchu a sacred city", Lima, 1983.

CACERES, Efrain, "Si Crees, los Apus Te Curen", Centro de Medicina Andina, Cuzco, 1988. CAMACHO PAREDES, Darwin, "The True of Machu Picchu", Cusco, 2001.

CARRION, Rebecca, "El culto al agua en el antiguo Peru", Revista del Museo Nacional de Antropologia y Arqueologia, Lima, 1995.

CHAMPI MONTEROSO, Piedad, "Informe Anual de Investigacion arqueológica de Patallaqta" (Ministerio de Cultura Cusco), Cusco, 2005.

CHOQUE CENTENO, Mercedes Gloria, "Informe Anual de Obra Parque Arqueológico de Machu Picchu C.A. de Huayllabamba" (Ministerio de Cultura Cusco), Cusco, 2006.

COBO, Bernabe, "Historia del nuevo mundo", Madrid, 1956, 1653.

CUBA GUTIERREZ, Cosme, "MACHU PICCHU IN INKA HISTORY", GRAFIKA PRESS, 2007.

DOBSON, Jim, in la Revista "Forbes", "Will a Hidden Treasure Chamber Discovered Under Machu Picchu Finally Be Revealed?", July 26, 2016.

ESPINOZA SORIANO, Waldemar "LOS INCAS. Economia Sociedad y Estado en la Era del Tahuantinsuyo", AMARU Editores, Lima, 1997.

FLORES OCHOA, Jorge A., Roberto, SAMANEZ ARGUMEDO, Luis Federico, BARREDA MURILLO, "From Myth to History. Art and Treasures of Peru Collection", Banco Credito del Cuzco, Peru, 2007.

GUAMAN POMA DE AYALA, Phelipe, "Nueva crónica y buen gobierno", Paris, 1936, 1600. HEMMING, John, "The Conquest of the Incas", London, 1970.

HUARCAYA, Francisco, "Informe Anual de Investigacion Arqueologica C.A. SALAPUNKU PANM - MAPI / Sector I, Tomo I, II, III y IV" (Ministerio de Cultura Cusco), Cusco, 2008.

FROST, Peter, "Exploring Cusco" (4th Edition), Lima, 2005.

GARCILASO DE LA VEGA, Inca, "Comentarios Reales", Ed. Mercurio, Volumes I, II, III. 1609. NATIONAL INSTITUTE OF CULTURE (Lima) / NATIONAL INSTITUTE OF CULTURE (Cusco),

"Master Plan of the Historic Sanctuary of Machu Picchu" - Summary, Lima, 2005.

JAMIN, Thierry, "Machu Picchu and the secret chamber", Jungle Doc Productions, France, March 2020.

KAUFFMANN DOIG, Federico, "MACHU PICCHU, Sortilegio en piedra", Volume I, II, Universidad Alas Peruanas, Lima, 2014.

KENDALL, Ann, "Architecture and planning at the Incas sites in the Cusichaca área", Berlin, 1974.

LIZARRAGA VALENCIA, Romulo, CUMES, Carol, "Journey to Machu Picchu", USA, 1999. MACERA, Pablo, "Historia del Peru", Lima, 1983.
MORH CHAVEZ KAREN L., "The Archaeology of Marcavalle / An early horizon site in the Valley of Cusco, Peru", Lima, 1980.
PARDO, Luis A., "Historia y arqueologia del Cusco", Cusco, 1957. REINHARD, Johan, "Machu Picchu / The Sacred Center", Lima, 1991.
ROZAS, Washington, "Los Paqo en Q'eros", Flores, J. & Nuñez del Prado, J., editors, "Q'ero:
El Ultimo Ayllu Inka", Centro de Estudios Andinos Cuzco, Cuzco, 1983. ROSTWOROWKI, Maria, "Pachacutec", Lima, 1980.
ROSTWOROWKI, Maria, "Historia del Tahuantinsuyo", Lima, 1988.
SCHLESINGER, Jr Arthur. ISRAEL Fred L. "The Ancient Incas", CHRONICLES FROM NATIONAL GEOGRAPHIC, CHELSEA HOUSE PUBLISHERS, Philadelphia, 1999.
TAMAYO HERRERA, José, "Historia General del Cusco. Una Historia Regional desde el periodo Litico hasta el Año 2000", Municipality of Cusco, 1992.
TOVAR CAYO, Jose Luis, "Informe Anual de los Conjuntos arqueológicos de PHUYUPATAMARKA y SAYAQMARKA" (Ministry of Culture of Cusco), Cusco, 1996.
VARCARCEL, Luis, "Machu Picchu: The Famous Archaeological Monument of Peru" (7th edition), Editorial Salesiana, Lima, 1979.

THE INCA TRAIL TO MACHU PICCHU

Printed in Great Britain
by Amazon